Dedicated to
My late husband & best friend

Francesco Costantini
December 3, 1937 - December 24, 2013

ACKNOWLEDGMENTS

Italian Moms – Spreading Their Art To Every Table has been a labor of love filled with passion and tears. After the death of my husband, I realized that he would be missed by so many people by the display of love that was shared with him in the last few weeks of his life. Their visits with him showed me just how much the special talent he had shared meant to our family, friends, and his clients. Francesco was an artist in his own right; a skilled carpenter who created art that people have the pleasure of enjoying in their lives day after day. His work will be the stage for families to create memories and I want to do the same as families gather together around the table. I will not live forever, and I am sure there are great–grandchildren I will not meet, but with these recipes, they will be able to make me a part of their celebrations and memories.

I have enjoyed working with my son Frank, and daughter Nadia in bringing this book to life. It has not been easy, but it brought us together in a time when a worthwhile distraction was of the upmost importance. It was in sense a therapy that I needed desperately. It has given me a new purpose. In addition to my family, there are several individuals to whom I owe my personal gratitude.

I would like to thank Bryan Bechtel, my narrative writer. This young man sat with me on many occasions, listening to my stories through many tears and has brought them to life throughout the vignettes of this book. I first met Bryan when he came to a garage sale I was having, selling the collection of tools Francesco had accumulated over 40 years. He purchased my husband's most prized table saw, something he used constantly to create the impossible for so many. We learned of Bryan's profession, and after a short conversation he offered to help us with this project. Was it a coincidence? I don't think so. I believe a higher power brought Bryan into our lives to give us the assistance we needed to complete this project.

I would also like to thank the power of the internet that brought Mary Bianchetti, a woman I have yet to meet in person. She reached out to us offering her marketing expertise and has walked us through this process every step of the way. I ask myself, why? Why are these strangers, people who have never met me, being so kind? Then I realized that there are still good people in our world, those who see supporting each other as a part of life, and for this I am very grateful. To my editors, Claire Boughan–Locke, Milena Trosini and Nancy Sullivan. You are so kind for offering your time to check and recheck that I did not leave out a single detail.

Finally, to my friends, Gabriella Versano and Gina Tulli, who not only shared recipes, but also have given me their shoulders to cry on and for encouraging me to keep going day by day. I am forever grateful.

HAZELNUT BALLS

SEE PAGE 228

CONTENTS

INTRODUCTION

Being the one responsible for putting food on my family's table gives me a sense of pride, and it is how I express my love for those who gather at my table. Because it is a matter of love and affection when I prepare meals, I tend to add ingredients on whim and whimsy rather than according to instruction. That is to say, I do not typically follow formulas, but rather instinct and experience. I do not record my recipes (actually, I have never in my life written one down until now), nor do I ever really look at other recipes for inspiration. I suspect many home cooks operate the same way: add a little bit of this or that and adjust according to taste.

So, why am I now gathering a collection of recipes that have been in my family for generations? In part, it is because of the name of the coauthor on this book, my son Frank. I have happily spent a lifetime preparing food and caring for my family, and so when he approached me with the idea of recording my recipes, I saw it as an opportunity to spend time with my son while enjoying a lifelong passion. It would be a blessing if anything, that what I have learned over the years could be useful to someone else.

There is perhaps a notion of legacy in these pages, as well. The recipes I present here have gathered in my memory for decades; each one has at one time or another been prepared for my family or loved ones. I am humbled to remember those moments of satisfaction my children or my husband (or whomever I was cooking for) felt when they ate my food. And so, I associate memories with the meals I have prepared, and this collection is a way to honor those memories.

The other aspect of legacy is that now that I have this collection, I have something tangible to pass forward to my children and to others who may be interested in reading about the art of Italian cooking. I was not fortunate enough to have such a guide when I learned to cook, and so if these recipes are at all a help to the at–home cook, I am more than happy to share a few of my secrets.

Where do all these recipes come from? From a lifetime spent in the kitchen, taking simple ingredients and transforming them into something greater. In a way, each of the recipes is a story. To me, each meal is an amalgamation of what may seem like ordinary ingredients—tomatoes, basil, meats and cheeses—but when they are put together in just the right way, and when done so with love and affection, they blend to create something much greater.

And isn't this an interesting analogy for life? If one takes care to nurture the essential things–family, friends and loved ones—they become the sustenance of life, capable of nourishing your soul and feeding your every pleasure.

My appreciation for food derives quite literally from spending time with family. I first entered the kitchen as a very young girl at the hip of my Aunt Ida who was a celebrated chef and caterer in the province of Teramo, located in the Abruzzo region of Italy.

Whenever she was called on to prepare a meal for a wedding or party, or if someone asked her to make dinner for their family, my father would send me to help Aunt Ida. Was it because I was an expert sous chef? Was I particularly handy with a knife? Did I have an extensive knowledge of cooking and the delicate touch needed to create a meal from a pile of ingredients? No, it wasn't for any of these reasons. In fact, I was quite the novice, a very young child who could not even reach the countertop even if I stood on the very tips of my toes.

No Aunt Ida allowed me to go along to help because she didn't trust anyone with her secret recipes. On many occasions we worked before sunrise, hidden away so no one would see what exactly she was using to prepare her masterpieces. I was simply a confidant, perhaps a bit shy, but also perhaps a bit too naïve to know what I was doing. I was the perfect patsy, unwilling or unable to really spill the beans on my aunt's recipes.

In fact, I owe a tremendous amount to Aunt Ida because she instilled in me a love for cooking and taught me the skills I would later hone in my family's kitchen. We lived humbly and simply in our small village of Poggio Valle on a farm where my parents, Alfredo and Maria Fantozzi, cultivated all the food we shared at our table. Truth be told, my father was not much of a farmer, but he was good enough to provide for the needs of our family.

Perhaps that was important training—we had just enough to get by, we could not want for much more, but at the same time, nothing could be wasted. This taught me that each ingredient is a precious thing to be cherished and treasured, a prized commodity that must be handled with care.

I recall fondly the memories of my early years in Poggio Valle, a simple community of 25 or so families. It is where I learned the importance of family and it is where I would one day meet my beloved husband, Francesco. I was stricken the moment he rode into town on a motorcycle looking for work as a bricklayer. Having already been promised to another, I tried to ignore him, but Francesco wooed me through a series of conversations late at night through a neighbor's kitchen window. We were young and in love.

Perhaps we did not know much better, but fate brought us to the same place; and so, when we married, I felt like we were simply soul mates following our destiny.

Less than a year after we were married, Francesco was conscripted into a mandatory term in the army, which would separate us for 18 months. But before Francesco's departure, I became pregnant with our first child, Nadia. These were joyous years, and we were proud of our growing family.

There was, however, one source of disagreement between us. Francesco desperately wanted to live in America, a land I had little desire to even visit. Although I was born in Italy, I had the ability to apply for US citizenship because my mother had gained citizenship and lived in the United States prior to my birth. I had little interest in doing this, but alas, I finally gave in and decided to at least try living in America.

In April 1961, our family began the voyage from Italy to a new homeland. As a 23–years-old, I boarded the SS Independence for an arduous 9–day journey. Because Nadia's paperwork got held up in bureaucracy, Francesco and my daughter would have to come later. This was actually quite a frightening thing to me: I would be a foreigner traveling to a new land without my family nearby to comfort me. I had never traveled outside of Abruzzo, let alone another country. It was the longest 9 days of my life. But Francesco surprised me; he had secured the proper paperwork and had flown to America ahead of my arrival, and we were quickly reunited. I do recall having Francesco promise me that he would not fly with our daughter on a plane all the way to America. But the joy of seeing him when I arrived in Philadelphia tempered my frustration with him. Besides, the years have passed, and these small details tend to fade away in the face of happier memories.

I will admit that life was strange in America where I learned English watching episodes of I Love Lucy. I often got lonely because, while Francesco, my brother, his wife and cousins who had come before us, all had jobs to go to, I was alone in the apartment with Nadia. We were fortunate to settle in Philadelphia among a community of like–minded Italian immigrant families and as time passed, I began to make some friends. At times, it could feel very much like Poggio Valle a collection of families sharing in the struggle of trying to provide for the necessities of family. Yet, I still believed that our stay in America would be temporary and that we would soon return to the more familiar confines of Italy. My hopes for a return to Italy were dashed after my second child, Agnes, was born with a medical disability. She received excellent care in America, and I felt she had to stay close to her doctors and nurses. And so, I had to resign myself to a new reality – I would never return to live in Italy full time.

Despite never having much money, we were a happy family, and I took great pride in being able to prepare meals for my family and care for their basic needs. We would be blessed with another child, a son, Frank, and we would continue to make many great friends. I would also find salvation after the death of my daughter when fate and chance brought me to the doors of the Don Guanella School run by the Archdiocese of Philadelphia, where I found a career caring for children with special needs as a housekeeper and cook. Over 35 years later, I still work with these lovely children, and it gives me a sense of purpose and belonging to be in their company. They were my salvation after I lost my daughter, and again now that Francesco has also been taken from me. They need me, and I need them.

I have seen a great many things in my life from unbelievable joy and happiness to moments of sadness and hardship; through it all, I have found meaning and purpose in my family and my ability to care for them in the best way I know how. I was blessed with a talent for cooking, and so I am honored and humbled to share these skills now in this collection of recipes. I would like to dedicate this collection to my beloved Francesco. I was fortunate to spend over 55 years with him, building a family and living an extraordinary life together.

When I say that preparing food is a responsibility, it means so much more than that. It means caring for family, the kinship of friends, and the sharing of good times despite life's struggles. It means giving a little of yourself each time you put food on a plate to share with whomever has gathered at your table. It means taking the time and care needed to lovingly take a collection of ingredients and shape them into something more. Food is a way to tell a story, to share yourself, to create, to care for, to nurture. Food … is love.

ABOUT ABRUZZO

The region of Abruzzo sits east in Italy's long, narrow peninsula. About two-thirds of the region is mountainous, but also boarders the coastline along the Adriatic Sea. It is considered part of Southern Italy.

The province's economy is supported by the farming of local fruits, olives, and livestock. The ventricina teramana is produced between the mountains and hills of the Gran Sasso; an especially fat salami which is fine-grained and spreadable, light in color and spicy. The Millefiori mountain honey is especially tasty. Extra-virgin olive oil, also harvested in Abruzzo, seasons many typical dishes of my region. One of the most recognizable symbols of the Teramo Province's cuisine is the sheep arrosticini, little pieces of mutton cooked on a skewer. Abruzzese lamb in general is considered superior in flavor to other meats and lamb found elsewhere because of the animals' mountain-grazed diets rich in herbs. The steep mountains in part of the countryside lend themselves well to sheep and goat herding. Pork is an omnipresent meat staple and a particular favorite in Italian sausages as well as smoked and cured meat products. Chicken, turkey and wild fowl are plentiful. Parsley, rosemary and garlic hold prominent places in the flavoring of dishes.

Also famous in my region are the spreadable sausages flavored with nutmeg, liver, garlic and spices. They are made with large pieces of fat and lean pork, pressed, seasoned and encased in the dehydrated stomach of the pig itself. It is then sealed in jars, and serves as lunch with some fresh bread for those working in the fields. Mortadella is another famous product from my region, a small cured meat, with a longish oval-shape. Inside, the meat is married with white columns of fat. They are generally sold in pairs. Together, they are about as big as two cupped hands put together. Another name for Mortadella in Italian is "coglioni di mulo," or donkey's balls.

Several flavors and dishes rise far above the others to help define Abruzzese cuisine. In this cheese-loving region, mozzarella and scamorza are very important to the dairy market. Both are cow's milk cheeses, they are mild, creamy and sweet with a smooth texture that allows them to hold up equally well in baked dishes or on their own as table cheeses.

Although tasty, these cheeses play second fiddle to the Pecorino cheese made from sheep's milk in the most remote mountain towns, like that of my hometown Poggio Valle.

MAZZARELLE
DI FEGATO

SEE PAGE 26

Ragù is quintessentially Abruzzese, and refers to a generalized term to any type of meat-based sauce. Ragù is heavily associated with the cooking of Southern Italy as well, and seems to have begun its migration southward from this particular region. Pairing perfectly with hearty Abruzzese dishes is a locally-loved table wine, Montepulciano d'Abruzzo, made from Montepulciano grapes grown in Tuscany but employed heavily in the winemaking of the Abruzzo region. From the basics – olives, grapes and pasta – to the bizarre – lamb's intestines cooked with intentionally rotten cheese – Abruzzese cuisine is beginning to again capture the attention of cooks around the world seeking to return to the heart and soul of Italian cooking.

The most flavorful local recipes started out as necessity, ways to use readily available ingredients and leftovers to produce food that was both practical and pleasant. Almost every edible part of any ingredient is utilized somehow in Abruzzese cooking. Nothing is wasted, and little is lost. The people are frugal, but hearty. Today's Abruzzese dishes hold true to their past, and marry earthy flavors with spices to make the palate sing. Isn't that what we really want from Italian food? It is how I have prepared meals for my family and friends for decades. Along the coast, it is possible to taste the seafood hors d'oeuvres, typical of Giulianova; it is based on prawns, squids, clams and sole. On Christmas Eve it is traditional to cook stockfish, a very tasty dish based with oil and spices that requires hours of preparation.

Many travelers came and went through the center of Italy, through Abruzzo's provinces of Teramo, Pescara, Chieti and L'Aquila. Some left influences from distant parts of Italian culture and from other countries as well. Travelers and pilgrims came and went, and some stayed, lending more and more diversity to the heritage of Abruzzo, and to its cuisine. The region's history of variety has culminated in contemporary times to produce some of Italy's most unique and interesting dishes.

Today, the Abruzzo region of Italy lies somewhat outside the country's normal tourist route, and many travelers who come choose to visit the beaches of Pescara and Giulianova. Other travelers take the more traditional tourist attractions in the Lazio region (home to the country's capital of Rome) adjacent to Abruzzo over the Gran Sasso Mountains or a pilgrimage to the shrine of San Gabrielle in Isola, my husband's hometown.

Abruzzo, then, is a perfect destination in which to discover the time-tested flavors of old-world Italian food unencumbered by the normal tourist trappings. While Abruzzo is fascinating year-round, August is full of festivals, family gatherings, and food preparation for the winter months. It is when we prepare our most important pantry ingredient, tomato sauce!

COOKING TIPS

- Always have salt and pepper close by when you are cooking. Sometimes you need to be the judge if your dish needs an extra pinch of these cooking essentials.

- When you are sautéing or roasting always have a cup of water handy. If your pan looks dry, add ¼–cup of water at a time to keep your dish from drying out.

- When boiling water for pasta add a tablespoon of olive oil to prevent the pasta from sticking together. And never discard all of your pasta water.

- When making egg–based pasta dough, depending on the size of the eggs, you may need to add some extra flour. If the dough is too moist, add flour; if it is too dry, add water.

- Every oven is different. When cooking something for the first time, watch it closely; you may have to adjust the cooking time or temperature to fit your oven.

- Throughout my recipes I mention Pecorino Romano cheese because most grocery chains carry it. However, if you can find Pecorino d'Abruzzo, I recommend you purchase it. It is from my hometown, and has a much stronger flavor.

- Do not get discouraged the first few times you attempt to bake bread and the dough does not rise. Making bread is difficult and takes practice. You cannot control the activeness of the yeast and the room temperature plays an important role in the success of dough rising.

- When preparing a dish that requires frying, always place it in the oven afterwards and bake for a few minutes to reduce the greasiness of the dish.

- Always use fresh ingredients. Plan to visit the market the day you plan on cooking.

- Make a list and check it twice.

- Serving sizes – I have omitted serving sizes for some dishes and cookies. Sometimes you cannot judge how much your guests will take! Rest assured, being Italian, my serving size for 4–6 people, may translate to 8–10 people. But that is okay, just offer your guests seconds, and serve it to them before they have a chance to say no.

- Visit my website for more detailed step by step instructions and videos of me preparing my favorite dishes at www.italianmomscooking.com

ANTIPASTI

CLAMS PROVENCAL

INGREDIENTS

- 40 littleneck clams
- 1 cup dry white wine
- 1 cup fresh parsley, chopped
- ¼ cup olive oil
- 1½ cups Italian–style bread crumbs
- ¼ cup scallions, chopped
- 1 cup heavy cream
- 2 small tomatoes, peeled and chopped
- ½ cup pancetta or bacon, minced
- 4 tablespoons butter, softened
- Fresh Parmesan cheese, grated
- Salt and fresh black pepper to taste

DIRECTIONS

Wash and brush the clams in a strainer under cold water.

In a large saucepan, combine wine, scallions, parsley, and clams, cover with a lid and let cook on medium to high heat until all the clams have opened. If you plan on serving over pasta, double the clams used, and set some opened clams aside for decoration. Remove the clams from their shells; be careful not to break them apart. Save ¼ cup of the broth from the pan for later. Set the separate clams off to the side.

Heat the olive oil in a large skillet and add the breadcrumbs. Sauté the breadcrumbs for 2-4 minutes and blend them thoroughly with the olive oil. Add the tomatoes, salt and pepper to taste, and sauté for another 2-4 minutes. Finally add the pancetta or bacon and sauté for 2 minutes. In a separate bowl, add the clam broth you saved to the heavy cream and blend thoroughly.

"This can be served as an antipasto or served over linguine as a pasta course."
- Elisa

Preheat oven to 350 degrees F.

Place a layer of the breadcrumb mixture in six buttered scallop dishes, or an 8 x 8-inch glass casserole dish. Place a layer of clams on top of the breadcrumb base and cover with a layer of the cream mixture. Add a second layer of the breadcrumb mixture. Brush the tops with butter and add the remaining cream to the top. Sprinkle some additional breadcrumbs on top and place in the oven. Bake for 10 minutes or until lightly browned on top, remove and set aside for 5 minutes. Garnish with some chopped parsley and Parmesan cheese.

PASTA OPTION:

Add the heavy cream and clam broth to the breadcrumb mixture and mix with a wooden spoon. Add the clams and simmer until the pasta is ready. Strain the pasta, and pour the clam sauce over the pasta. Garnish with the clams still in the shells you set aside earlier. Sprinkle evenly with some fresh chopped parsley, Parmesan cheese, fresh ground black and crushed red pepper on top.

PHILLY CHEESESTEAK SANDWICHES
PANINI DI BISTECCA

INGREDIENTS

- ¾ pound Beef Top Chipped Round Steak
- 2 teaspoons vegetable oil
- 2 small yellow onions, sliced
- 1 teaspoon crushed red pepper
- Pinch of salt and fresh black pepper
- 4 slices American cheese
- ¼ cup fresh Mozzarella cheese
- ¼ cup roasted red peppers
- Fresh Italian long rolls

"I call these sandwiches by this name now, but I have been preparing them since I was a teenager, when I would pack sandwiches for a picnic. I always have the ingredients to whip up these quick and easy sandwiches. I feed them to my son, when he gets restless, which tells me he needs a snack. You can also prepare these as antipasta, by slicing them down for everyone at the table to enjoy!" - Elisa

DIRECTIONS

Preheat oven to 350 degrees F.

In a medium–sized frying pan, add the oil and sliced onions. Sauté the onions for about 5 minutes. When they begin to show some darkening in color add the beef, salt, and black pepper.

Allow the meat and onions to cook through for 10 minutes. While the meat is simmering, slice the roll and spoon out half of the center to make room for the filling and place on oven rack to toast for 5 minutes, then remove from the oven.

Add the cheese to the pan and reduce the heat. As the cheese melts, add the roasted red peppers and mix with a wooden spoon. Remove from heat and fill the roll.

FRIED RISOTTO BALLS
ARANCINI

SERVES 4 PEOPLE (2 EACH)

INGREDIENTS

- 3 cups cooked risotto
- ¼ cup Parmesan cheese, grated
- ¼ cup Pecorino Romano cheese, grated
- 3 eggs
- ½ cup fresh mozzarella, cubed
- 3 cups Italian-style breadcrumbs
- 3 cups vegetable oil
- 1 cup fresh marinara sauce, see recipe under Sauces, pg.126
- A pinch of salt and fresh black pepper

DIRECTIONS

THE RISOTTO SHOULD BE PREPARED A DAY PRIOR TO MAKING YOUR ARANCINI.

Remove the risotto from the refrigerator. Combine the risotto, Parmesan, Pecorino Romano, mozzarella, and 1 egg in a medium bowl and use your hands to thoroughly combine the mixture. Form each arancini by taking a small portion of the mixture, the size of a small orange, squeezing it firmly into a nice round shape. Repeat this process to form 8 arancini. Whisk together the remaining 2 eggs. Dip each arancini in the eggs and then roll them in the bowl of breadcrumbs, shaking off any excess. Place them in the refrigerator for 15 minutes.

Preheat the oil over medium heat in a saucepan. The oil should be 4 inches high in the saucepan. Reduce the heat of the oil slightly, and add 2 or 3 of the breaded arancini to the saucepan and fry them until golden brown and cooked throughout, approximately 5-7 minutes. You can also use a deep fryer.

Use a slotted spoon to remove the fried arancini from the pot and transfer them to a paper towel-lined plate. Repeat the frying process with the remaining arancini. Serve the arancini warm with a side of warm marinara sauce.

VEGETABLE PIE

TORTA DI VERDURE

"This is a type of Stromboli, that we prepare for special celebrations. I tend to use broccoli rabe, but you can use spinach, asparagus, traditional broccoli or a mixture of a few vegetables." – Elisa

INGREDIENTS

PASTRY DOUGH:

- 3 cups all-purpose flour
- ⅓ cup extra virgin olive oil
- ¾ cup water
- 1 teaspoon salt

FILLING:

- 2 cups of green vegetables, boiled
- 2 cups of ricotta cheese, drained
- ⅓ cup of Italian- style breadcrumbs
- 1 garlic clove, chopped
- 1 egg
- ¼ cup of fresh Parmesan and Pecorino Romano cheeses, grated
- Salt and pepper to taste

DIRECTIONS

Preheat oven to 350 degrees F.

Place all dough ingredients in a stand mixer. Using the dough hook, knead until the dough is smooth and combined. Wrap in plastic and refrigerate while you make the filling. To create the filling, mix the vegetables and the ricotta cheese in a large mixing bowl. Add the egg, grated cheeses, breadcrumbs, garlic and salt and pepper and mix well.

Unwrap your dough from the plastic and divide it into two equal parts. Using a rolling pin, roll out each dough ball on a lightly floured surface, to create two circles, the size of a dinner plate. Place your first circle on a baking sheet or pizza pan and evenly spread the mixture leaving 1 inch from the edges. Sprinkle the filling with some additional Parmesan cheese. Cover with the second circle of dough. Seal the edges with your hands, and then use a fork to press down the edges.

Place a small bowl in the middle of the pie and press lightly to make an indentation. Use your fork to press lightly. Cut the dough into strips approximately 1-inch wide, keeping it attached at the center. Twist each slice and continue the twisting until each slice is twisted. Bake the pie for 30 minutes or until golden. Remove from oven and cool on a wire rack. Serve warm.

BRUSCHETTA BALSAMICO

SERVES 8 PEOPLE

INGREDIENTS

- 8 fresh tomatoes, diced
- ½ cup fresh basil, chopped
- ¼ cup fresh Parmesan cheese, grated
- 2 garlic cloves, minced
- 1 tablespoon balsamic vinegar
- 1 tablespoon olive oil
- A pinch of salt and fresh black pepper
- 1 loaf fresh Italian bread

DIRECTIONS

In a bowl, toss together the tomatoes, basil, Parmesan cheese, and garlic. Mix in the balsamic vinegar, olive oil, salt, and pepper. Serve on toasted bread slices or in a bowl with warm fresh baked bread.

CAPRESE SALAD
INSALATA CAPRESE

SERVES 4–6 PEOPLE

INGREDIENTS

- 3 large ripe tomatoes
- 1 pound fresh mozzarella cheese
- 1 bunch fresh basil
- ¼ cup olive oil
- 2 tablespoons red wine vinegar
- Pinch of salt

DIRECTIONS

Slice the tomatoes and mozzarella cheese into ¼-inch thick slices. Layer alternating slices of tomatoes, then a basil leaf and then mozzarella on a serving dish. Drizzle the salad with the olive oil and drips of the vinegar. Garnish with a pinch of salt and serve with prosciutto- wrapped bread sticks.

CAPRESE
SALAD
———
INSALATA
CAPRESE

CHILLED ITALIAN SEAFOOD SALAD

FRUTTI DI MARE FREDDO

SERVES 8 PEOPLE

INGREDIENTS

FOR THE SALAD:

- 1½ pounds calamari rings
- 1½ pounds small fresh shrimp, peeled and deveined
- 1½ pounds small scallops
- 3 cups dry white wine
- 4 bay leaves, whole
- 3 garlic cloves, minced
- 3 lemons
- 1 cup celery, chopped
- 1 cup yellow & red peppers, chopped

FOR THE DRESSING:

- 2 cups olive oil
- 1 cup lemon juice
- 3 garlic cloves, minced
- ½ cup fresh parsley, chopped
- ½ cup fresh basil, chopped
- 2 teaspoons crushed red pepper
- 2 lemons, sliced
- Salt and Pepper to taste

DIRECTIONS

In a stockpot, combine 10 cups of water, white wine, bay leaves, and crushed garlic. Cut the lemons in half and squeeze the juice into the mixture. Drop the lemons into the pot, then bring the mixture first to a boil. Reduce the heat to medium low. Add the shrimp to the pot, and cook for 2 minutes and remove from the pot with straining spoon and set aside in a bowl. Add the calamari to the pot for 2 minutes. Remove from the pot with the straining spoon and add to the bowl as well. Repeat the same procedure for the scallops, cook for 2 minutes.

Once you have finished adding all the fish to the bowl, add the chopped celery and peppers. Prepare the dressing, and toss with the fish. Cover and let marinate 6 hours in the refrigerator. Just before serving, give it a toss, and garnish with fresh black pepper, chopped parsley, basil, and lemon wedges. Serve at room temperature.

CHILLED ITALIAN SEAFOOD SALAD

FRUTTI DI MARE FREDDO

ROASTED RED PEPPERS

PEPERONI ARROSTI

SERVES 4–6 PEOPLE

INGREDIENTS

- 4 large red peppers
- ¼ cup olive oil
- ¼ cup fresh parsley, chopped
- 2–3 garlic cloves, chopped
- ½ teaspoon salt

DIRECTIONS

Preheat oven to 400 degrees F.

Cut peppers into quarters and remove the stem and seeds. Place the peppers skin side up on a baking sheet and bake for 1 hour. The peppers should be wrinkled. Remove and cool to room temperature. Peel away the skin and cut into ¼–inch strips. Place peppers in a bowl and add the olive oil, parsley, garlic and salt. Mix well, cover bowl with plastic wrap and set aside to marinate until ready to serve.

ROASTED RED PEPPERS
───────────────
PEPERONI ARROSTI

FRIED POLENTA
POLENTA FRITTA

"You should prepare the polenta for this dish the day before you plan to fry and serve. This dish has a kick, so I hope you like spicy." - Elisa

INGREDIENTS

- 1 pound Italian Sausage, sweet or hot, depending on your audience
- 2 cups yellow Italian Polenta
- 6 cups water
- 1 teaspoon salt
- 2 teaspoons red pepper flakes
- ¼ cup fresh Parmesan cheese, grated
- ¼ cup fresh Pecorino Romano cheese, grated
- 1 teaspoon fresh black pepper
- 2 cups vegetable oil

FOR THE GARNISH AND DIPPING:

- 2 cups fresh marinara sauce, see recipe under Sauces, pg.126
- ¼ cup fresh Parmesan and Pecorino Romano, shredded

DIRECTIONS

Bring the water to a boil in a large stockpot. Add 2 teaspoons of salt and gradually whisk in the polenta. Reduce the heat to low and cook until the mixture thickens and the polenta is tender but still very loose and creamy, stirring almost constantly for about 20-25 minutes.

Remove the sausage meat from the casing and crumble into the polenta in the saucepan. Add the cheese, pepper flakes, salt, and pepper. Continue to stir continuously for 10 minutes.

Remove and pour Polenta mixture into a greased 13 x 9 x 2-inch glass casserole pan and refrigerate for at least 4 hours. I recommend you prepare this a day before, and refrigerate overnight.

Once you are ready to fry, preheat the oil on medium high heat in a skillet. Remove the polenta from the refrigerator, and cut the polenta into 2-inch by 1-inch slices. Reduce the heat slightly, and place 2-4 pieces into the oil, frying and turning using tongs, until all sides are golden brown, roughly 3-4 minutes for each side. Remove and dry on a paper towel-covered wire rack. Garnish with the shredded cheese and serve with a side of sauce.

STUFFED RED PEPPERS

PEPERONI ROSSI RIPIENI

"Traditionally I use long red peppers, but you can use red, green, and yellow peppers to create a festive presentation." - Elisa

SERVES 8 PEOPLE

INGREDIENTS

- 8 medium–sized red peppers
- 1 cup chopped onion
- ½ cup fresh Italian parsley, chopped
- ½ cup celery, chopped
- 1½ cups eggplant, chopped
- 3 ounce boneless ham steak or 3 ounce of prosciutto, chopped
- 1 cup mozzarella cheese shredded
- 2 eggs
- 1 cup Italian–Style breadcrumbs

DIRECTIONS

Preheat oven to 350 degrees F. While oven is heating, add the olive oil to a medium-sized saucepan and heat.

In a large mixing bowl, combine the onions, parsley, celery, eggplant, and choice of meat. Mix thoroughly and then add to the saucepan. Sauté the mixture for 10 minutes. In a small mixing bowl, beat the eggs, and add the mozzarella cheese and breadcrumbs mix thoroughly.

Add the egg mixture to the saucepan and cook for another 30 seconds mixing continuously. Remove from heat and set aside. Remove the top of the peppers with a knife and remove the seeds. Fill each pepper with the stuffing mixture and place in a baking dish. Add two tablespoons of water and two tablespoons of olive oil to the baking dish and bake for 1 hour.

CHEESE BALLS
ABRUZZESE POLPETTINE

SERVES 8 PEOPLE

INGREDIENTS:

- 4 cups Italian–style breadcrumbs
- ¼ cup fresh parsley, finely chopped
- 2 garlic cloves, minced
- 8 eggs
- 10 ounces Parmesan cheese, grated
- 10 ounces Pecorino Romano cheese, grated
- 1 cup olive oil
- 2 cups fresh marinara sauce see recipe under Sauces, pg.126

DIRECTIONS:

In a bowl, mix the breadcrumbs, cheese and eggs. Complete the mixture by adding the garlic and parsley, and form the balls into the size of an olive to be fried. Place them in the refrigerator for 1 hour.

Heat the olive oil in a large frying pan. Once the oil is hot, add 4-6 of the cheese balls to the pan at a time and fry them until golden brown and cooked throughout, about 4-6 minutes.

Use a slotted spoon to remove the cheese balls from the pan and transfer them to a paper towel-lined plate. Repeat the frying process with the remaining balls. Serve the cheese balls warm with a side of warm marinara sauce you have already prepared.

SPINACH & ONION OMELET
FRITTATA DI SPINACI E CIPOLLE

SERVES 4–6 PEOPLE

INGREDIENTS

- 8 eggs
- 1 cup cooked spinach
- 1 cup onions, chopped
- 1 tablespoon olive oil
- ¼ cup Pecorino Romano cheese, shredded
- Salt and Pepper to taste

DIRECTIONS:

Beat the eggs in a glass–mixing bowl. Use a 10 or 12–inch nonstick pan with a thick bottom and rounded edges. Pour the olive oil onto a paper towel and grease the pan and heat on medium heat for 2–3 minutes.

Pour the beaten eggs into the pan; add the spinach and gently mix before the eggs begin to cook. Sprinkle half the cheese over the eggs, add a pinch of salt and pepper and let cook until firm. Flip the omelet over and sprinkle with the remaining cheese, and add another pinch of salt and pepper. Cook for an additional 2–3 minutes and remove from pan. Slice like a pie and serve warm or cold.

EGGPLANT MINI MEATBALLS

POLPETTE DI MELANZANE

SERVES 4–6 PEOPLE

INGREDIENTS:

- 5 large eggplants
- 2 large eggs, lightly beaten
- 2 cups Italian–style breadcrumbs
- ½ cup fresh Parmesan cheese, grated
- ¼ cup fresh Pecorino Romano cheese, grated
- 1 garlic clove, minced
- 1 teaspoon salt
- 1 teaspoon fresh black pepper
- ¼ cup fresh basil, finely chopped
- 1 cup olive oil
- 2 cups fresh marinara sauce for dipping, see recipe under Sauces, pg.126

DIRECTIONS:

Preheat oven to 400 degrees F.

Wash and peel the skin from the eggplant and place whole on a baking sheet lined with foil. Bake for approximately 45 minutes, turning once, until very soft, and remove from the oven. Slice and remove any seeds. Drain any remaining liquid from the eggplant using a strainer.

Place the eggplant into a large bowl and add the eggs, 1 cup breadcrumbs, cheese, garlic, salt, pepper and basil. Stir the ingredients together until mixed thoroughly. Place the other cup of breadcrumbs in a small bowl. Form the mixture into little balls the size of walnuts. Roll them between the palms of your hands and roll in the breadcrumbs. Line up the balls on a baking sheet and refrigerate for 1 hour.

Heat the olive oil in a large skillet over medium heat and add the balls to the hot oil a few at a time, without overcrowding the pan. Fry over medium heat, turning so all sides cook evenly to a golden brown color. Cooking time should be 3–5 minutes depending on your stove. Dry the balls on a paper towel–lined plate, then transfer to a serving platter and serve hot with the tomato sauce for dipping.

ZUCCHINI & RICOTTA FRITTERS

FRITTELLE DI ZUCCHINE E RICOTTA

SERVES 6–8 PEOPLE

INGREDIENTS:

- ¾ pounds fresh zucchini, coarsely shredded
- 2 garlic cloves, very thinly sliced
- 3 scallions, very thinly sliced
- ½ cup whole ricotta cheese, drained
- 2 large eggs, lightly beaten
- 1 lemon peel, grated
- 1 teaspoon salt and fresh black pepper
- ¾ cup all–purpose flour
- 1 cup olive oil, for frying
- Lemon wedges, for garnish

DIRECTIONS:

In a large bowl, combine the zucchini, garlic, scallions, ricotta, eggs, lemon zest, salt, and pepper. Mix well and then stir in the flour and blend. In a large skillet, heat the olive oil. Working in batches, add heaping tablespoons of the zucchini batter to the hot oil in a single layer. Be careful not to overcrowd the pan.

Fry over medium heat, turning once, until browned and crisp on each side, about 3 minutes total. Drain the fritters on a paper towel–covered wire rack and serve immediately, with lemon wedges.

ITALIAN SAUSAGE & CHEESE FRITTATA

FRITTATA DI SALSICCIA E PECORINO

INGREDIENTS:

- ½ pound Italian sausage, crumbled
- 1 cup onion, thinly sliced
- ½ cup red bell pepper, thinly sliced
- ½ cup green bell pepper, thinly sliced
- 6 basil leaves, crumbled
- 4 large eggs
- ¼ cup olive oil
- ¼ cup heavy cream
- Salt and fresh black pepper to taste
- ¼ cup fresh Pecorino Romano cheese, grated

Heat 1 teaspoon of the olive oil in a 10- or 12-inch skillet. Add the sausage and sauté for 5 minutes over medium-high heat until it is no longer pink. Add the onion, bell peppers, salt, and pepper. Continue to sauté for 5 minutes, and then add the basil.

In a glass mixing bowl, beat the eggs, cream, cheese, and a pinch of salt and pepper. Add the hot sausage-pepper mixture, beating and stirring quickly to avoid scrambling the eggs, add some olive oil to the skillet and pour the mixture back into the skillet. Cook over medium heat 10 minutes, or until set and golden on the bottom. Flip the frittata and allow the other side to brown slightly.

Cut like a pizza into desired slice size. Serve hot or at room temperature.

STUFFED OLIVES
OLIVE RIPIENE

SERVES 4–6 PEOPLE

INGREDIENTS:

- 1 8–ounce jar large pitted green olives
- ¼ pound fresh Italian sausage, crumbled
- ½ cup ground veal
- ½ cup ground chicken or turkey
- 1 garlic clove, minced
- ½ cup all–purpose flour
- Pinch of nutmeg
- 2 tablespoons butter
- 3 tablespoons fresh Parmesan cheese, grated
- 2 eggs
- 2 cups Italian–style breadcrumbs
- ¼ cup olive oil
- 2 cups vegetable oil
- Salt and fresh black pepper to taste

DIRECTIONS:

In a medium skillet, sauté the olive oil, sausage, veal and chicken until the meat is no longer pink. Drain and place the meat in a bowl. Add 1 beaten egg, butter, garlic, cheese and nutmeg and mix thoroughly.

Drain the olives and rinse them under cold water. Stuff the olives with the mixture. Beat the remaining egg in a separate small bowl. Add the flour and breadcrumbs to separate bowls as well.

Heat the vegetable oil in a deep skillet over medium heat. Roll the olives, one by one, in the flour, then in the beaten egg, and then in the breadcrumbs. Drop the olives into the heated oil for 2–3 minutes, carefully rolling the olives so they fry evenly. Drain the olives on a paper towel–lined wire rack and transfer to your serving platter. Serve hot.

STUFFED PORTABELLO MUSHROOMS

INGREDIENTS

- 8 Portobello mushrooms caps
- 1 cup pancetta, cubed
- 1 cup fresh Parmesan cheese, shredded
- 2 eggs
- ½ cup Italian-style bread-crumbs
- 1 garlic clove, chopped
- ½ cup bell red pepper, chopped
- ¼ cup fresh parsley, chopped
- 2 tablespoons olive oil
- ¼ cup fresh Pecorino Romano cheese, grated
- ½ cup dry white wine
- Pinch of salt and fresh black pepper

DIRECTIONS:

Preheat oven at 400 degrees F.

Remove the stems and gently scrape the interior of the mushrooms, rinse under cold water, and pat dry. In a large bowl, beat the eggs, and then add the pancetta, ¾ cups of the Parmesan cheese, the breadcrumbs, garlic, bell pepper, parsley and olive oil and mix thoroughly.

Using a tablespoon, fill the mushroom caps. Top the mushrooms with the remaining Parmesan cheese and grated Pecorino cheese. Add a pinch of salt and black pepper to the tops. Line the mushrooms in a glass casserole dish and drizzle the white wine over the mushrooms. Bake for 20–25 minutes, until the tops are lightly brown and crispy. Remove and serve.

MAZZARELLE DI FEGATO

INGREDIENTS

- 2 pounds lamb liver or lamb meat
- 2 bunches fresh parsley
- 1½ pound scallions
- 1 bunch green garlic with stems
- 4 hearts Romaine lettuce
- Cooking twine
- ½ cup olive oil

DIRECTIONS:

Bring a large stockpot of water to a boil. Wash and dry off the liver. Slice the liver into pieces 1 inch wide and 3 inches long. Slice the scallions and green garlic, including the stems, into 3- inch slices. Chop the parsley into 3-inch bunches. Rinse and dry the lettuce and slice into 4- inch slices. Begin with 2 of the lettuce slices, overlapping them slightly, and then layer the remaining ingredients. Begin with a couple slices of the liver, then a handful of parsley, then a few scallion slices, and finally a few green garlic slices. Cover the filling with two additional leaves of lettuce. Using cooking twine, wrap the lettuce bundle very tightly, tucking in the ends to keep the filling from spilling out.

Drop the wraps into the boiling water and allow to cook for 45 minutes, until the lettuce is tender. Remove with a slotted spoon and adjust the twine if they appear loose. Heat the olive oil and a ladle of the water from the stockpot over medium heat, and add the wraps. Sauté over medium-low heat for 30 minutes. Remove, plate and serve at room temperature.

STUFFED PORTABELLO MUSHROOMS

FUNGHI PORTABELLO RIPIENI

SERVES 8 PEOPLE

SAUSAGE POPPERS

INGREDIENTS:

- 1 pound hot Italian sausage, crumbled
- ½ cup fresh Pecorino Romano or Parmesan cheese, grated
- ¼ cup fresh parsley, finely chopped including the stem
- 3 cups all–purpose flour or Bisquick

DIRECTIONS:

Preheat oven to 375 degrees F.

Combine all the ingredients in a glass mixing bowl and mix well with your hands. Take tablespoon size amounts of the mixture and roll into a ball and place on a waxed paper– covered cookie sheet 1–inch apart.

Bake for 20–25 minutes. Remove from oven and arrange on a serving platter.

STUFFED ARTICHOKES
CARCIOFI RIPIENI

INGREDIENTS:

- 4–6 medium sized artichokes
- 3 cups Italian–style breadcrumbs
- 2 tablespoons fresh parsley, chopped, including the stem
- 2 garlic cloves, finely chopped
- 1 lemon
- 1 teaspoon salt
- 2 cups fresh Pecorino Romano or Parmesan cheese, or a combination of the two, grated
- ½ teaspoon fresh black pepper
- ½ cup olive oil for the stuffing, and ¼ for the pot
- 4–5 cups vegetable stock

DIRECTIONS:

PREPARE THE STUFFING:
In a small bowl, add the breadcrumbs, garlic, parsley, olive oil, salt, and pepper and mix well with your hands. Refrigerate until ready to use.

PREPARE THE ARTICHOKES:
Wash the artichokes well, remove the tough outer leaves until you reach the lighter colored tender inner leaves, and then cut the stem off evenly so the artichoke will stand up. Using a knife, cut the point of the artichoke off flat at the height of the tips of the outermost leaves, then core it, removing the innermost leaves (just the innermost leaves above the heart) and any fuzz there may be in the center of the artichoke heart. Set aside the leaves removed, but discard the fuzz.

Next, spread the remaining leaves of the artichoke a bit with your fingers, and set the cored artichoke and the reserved leaves to soak in a bowl of water with the juice of a lemon.

When you've finished coring the artichokes, take the stems; if you look at a freshly cut surface you will see that the heart is lighter, and surrounded by a ring of darker green. Trim away the green outer parts, which are bitter. Julienne the white inner stems and add them to the reserved leaves and heart.

Remove the stuffing from the refrigerator, and spread the leaves of the artichokes like the petals of a flower and gently press the stuffing between them as well as into the central cavity.

Place artichokes in a heavy–bottomed pot over medium heat, and pour in ¼ cup of olive oil, then stand the artichokes upright in the pan. Allow them to cook for 5 minutes, then add the vegetable stock to cover the artichokes halfway up the sides and cover the pot tightly, reducing the heat to a slow simmer. Spoon some of the stock over the artichokes and simmer for 40–50 minutes, adding more stock as necessary to keep the artichokes from drying out.

Then uncover the pot and simmer until the water is evaporated; continue to baste the artichokes occasionally to keep them from sticking. Remove from the pot and serve.

STUFFED TOMATOES
POMODORI RIPIENI

INGREDIENTS

- 5–ounce can tuna in water, drained
- 4 fresh medium to large tomatoes
- 2 cups Italian–style breadcrumbs
- 2 tablespoons fresh parsley, chopped, including the stem
- 2 garlic cloves, finely chopped
- ½ cup olive oil
- ¼ cup fresh Pecorino Romano or Parmesan cheese, shredded
- Salt and fresh black pepper to taste

DIRECTIONS

Preheat oven to 350 degrees F.

In a glass mixing bowl, combine the breadcrumbs, parsley, garlic, olive oil, tuna fish and mix thoroughly. Slice the tops off of the tomatoes so you have a flat even top. Drain the juice. Add some salt to the centers of the tomatoes, and fill with the stuffing mixture. Sprinkle the tops with a pinch of pepper and the cheese. Line the tomatoes in a glass casserole dish and add some water to the bottom to prevent them from sticking. Bake for 30 minutes until the tomatoes are soft. Remove and serve.

SWEET FRIED POLENTA

FRITTI DI POLENTA DOLCE

INGREDIENTS:

- 1 portion of Italian Polenta, see my recipe in Pastas, pg.74 (do not add the cheese)
- 2 tablespoons vanilla extract
- 3 eggs, beaten
- 1 cup sugar
- ½ cup cinnamon
- 1 cup vegetable oil

DIRECTIONS:

Prepare 1 portion of my polenta recipe and add the vanilla extract while cooking. Pour polenta into a greased 13 x 9 x 2-inch glass casserole pan and refrigerate for at least 4 hours. I recommend you prepare this a day before, and refrigerate overnight.

Once you are ready to fry, preheat the oil on medium-high heat in a small stockpot. Remove the polenta from the refrigerator, and cut the polenta into 2-inch by 1-inch slices. Coat the pieces with the beaten egg. Roll in the sugar and cinnamon mixture and coat on both sides.

Reduce the heat slightly, and place 2-4 pieces into the oil frying and turning using tongs, until all sides are golden brown, roughly 3-4 minutes for each side. Remove and dry on a paper towel and line on a cookie sheet. Remove and transfer to a serving platter and serve hot. This is an excellent afternoon snack. To serve as a dessert, place over vanilla gelato and serve.

ZUCCHINI SQUARES

MAKES APPROX. 2 DOZEN SQUARES

INGREDIENTS:

- 3 cups fresh zucchini, peeled and shredded
- 4 eggs
- 1½ cups white onion, shredded
- ½ cup vegetable oil
- ½ cup Bisquick
- ½ cup fresh Parmesan cheese, grated
- 1 cup fresh Pecorino Romano cheese, grated

DIRECTIONS:

Preheat oven to 350 degrees F.

In a large mixing bowl, beat the eggs and oil. Add the Bisquick and blend. Drop the zucchini, cheeses, and onions into the mixture and fold through until you have an even mixture.

Grease a 13 x 9 x 2-inch glass pan, and pour the mixture into the pan. Bake for 1 hour until the top is golden brown. Remove from oven and let cook completely. Cut into 1½-inch by 1½- inch squares and arrange on serving platter. Insert cocktail toothpicks and serve.

STUFFED RED PEPPERS

PEPERONI ROSSI RIPIENI

SEE PAGE 21

FRIED ZUCCHINI
ZUCCHINE FRITTE

SERVES 4–6 PEOPLE

INGREDIENTS:

- 3 zucchini
- 2 eggs
- 1 cup all-purpose flour
- Pinch of salt
- Pinch of fresh black pepper
- 1 cup vegetable oil

DIRECTIONS:

Peel and slice the zucchini into ½ - inch pieces. Place the sliced zucchini into a bowl of cold water for 20-30 minutes. Beat the eggs in a bowl and in a separate bowl mix the flour, salt and pepper.

Heat the oil in a large skillet over medium heat. Once the oil has heated, one by one dip the slices of zucchini into the beaten eggs then drop into the flour mixture. Flip the zucchini to coat the slices evenly with flour. Place in the skillet and fry on each side for 3-4 minutes until golden brown.

Remove the slices from the skillet and place on a paper-towel covered wire rack and allow to cool for 5 minutes. Arrange on a platter, garnish with some additional salt and pepper and serve.

ITALIAN
CHICKEN WINGS

SERVES 4–6 PEOPLE

"Whenever my brother-in-law Mario comes to visit from Italy, I prepare these wings. They are his favorite afternoon snack. Now when we visit him, we have to pack 2-3 bottles of buffalo sauce for him." - Elisa

INGREDIENTS:

- 24 chicken wings and/or drummettes
- 2 cups all-purpose flour
- 4 garlic cloves, minced
- 1 teaspoon fresh oregano, finely chopped
- 1 teaspoon fresh parsley, finely chopped
- 1 teaspoon crushed red pepper
- Pinch of salt
- Pinch of fresh black pepper
- ¼ cup fresh Pecorino Romano cheese, grated
- 2 eggs
- 2 cups vegetable oil
- Buffalo sauce for garnish

DIRECTIONS:

Rinse the chicken pieces under cold water and set aside. Beat the eggs in a bowl and in a separate bowl mix the flour, garlic, oregano, parsley, red pepper, cheese, salt and black pepper.

Heat the oil in a large skillet over medium heat. Once the oil has heated, one by one dip the chicken pieces into the beaten eggs then drop into the flour mixture. Roll the chicken to coat the pieces evenly with flour. Place in the skillet and fry on each side for 4-5 minutes until golden brown.

Remove the chicken from the skillet with tongs and place on a paper-towel covered wire rack and allow to cool for 5 minutes. Arrange on a platter, garnish with some additional parsley, salt and black pepper and serve. You can also drizzle them with buffalo sauce for extra kick!

BREADS

ABOUT BREAD

Bread is traditionally associated with communal gathering, and rightly so. We think of breaking bread as a ceremony of bringing people together, of breaking down barriers, of uniting people around a table. It is shorthand for building relationships with strangers and strengthening the bonds of friendship with those we already know. Polite etiquette teaches us that we should pass bread around the table for everyone to share. And of course, there is the religious symbol of bread.

For an item with such a simple recipe list—yeast, flour, water, perhaps a little salt added—bread has many complex associations and evokes many emotions. Historians have found evidence of bread making as far back as 30,000 years ago, and today, bread plays an important role in many cultures around the world.

In the Italian diet, bread is an absolutely essential item that is produced in various forms, from rolls to flatbreads to loaves to pizza. Following are some traditional recipes I have acquired over the years from my own experiences making bread. Readers will be happy to know that they can find all of the ingredients used in this section at their local grocery store or market. I was not so fortunate when I learned to make bread.

In my village, most houses had a "casciona," a large freestanding wooden breadbox with a hinged top that functioned as the focal point of all bread making activities. On the inside of the box, at one end, old bread was used to make yeast for the new bread; in the middle of the storage part of the casciona, the proof of the new loaf would be left to rest. Prepared loaves were stored on the opposite end from where the yeast was started. And atop this bench-like construction is where we worked the loaves in their various stages.

But perhaps I am starting at the end of this story …

In our remote village, we grew wheat that we would harvest each year. After a period of cleaning and drying the harvested wheat, we would take it to a mill, which would separate out the usable flour (semolina) from the husks. The husks, the bran, would be saved to use as feed for livestock, and the course outer shell was useful as an abrasive for cleaning cooking pots and pans.

Harvesting wheat is hard work, but it is only the very first step in the process of making bread. Bread making is in some ways a continual cycle: leftover scraps from previous loaves were soaked in warm water to make the yeast to be used for the new loaves; that yeast is carefully added to flour that has been mixed with water (in the correct proportions, of course, which were always determined by an experienced eye—no measuring cups) and left to rise. This process of making the first proof would usually commence in very early hours of the morning, as early as 2:00 A.M. or 3:00 A.M. Awakening at this early hour was the responsibility of my brother Joe and I. We would prepare the first proof, so my mother would find the dough ready for use when she awoke in the morning.

The result of this first proofing is a mound of dough that was usually very large in size, about 25 pounds worth. It was laborious work to knead and work the dough; yet it was a delicate procedure, as good bread cannot be overworked, lest it become too elastic, yielding a final product that is chewy and rather tasteless. The balance in knowing to knead the dough just enough but not too much before ruining a loaf, can only come from experience.

The next step in this process occurs after the dough has rested for a few hours to rise a second time; then we would portion off the loaves and bake them in the stone hearth.

The last and perhaps most important part of this whole process is when we would get to finally eat the fruits of our labor. There is truly something to be said for being involved in each and every step of producing a loaf of bread, literally from the farm to the table.

Perhaps this all sounds a bit intimidating, but today, bread making is a much simpler process due to the availability of ingredients at local markets and stores. Yet the pride in the final product is by no means diminished, as it is a labor of love to produce a loaf of bread in any shape or size. The bread maker today may not literally be involved in each and every step of producing a loaf of bread: harvesting the wheat and milling it, producing flour, making the yeast, and shaping and baking the bread; and yet, making bread is a unique operation in the kitchen, for the baker's hands are, literally, involved in each and every step.

Making bread is to harness a living organism, the yeast, and to join it with the proper ingredients to produce a creation that is symbolic of sustenance, nourishment, and the affirmation of life. I firmly believe that anyone interested in preparing food should, at least once in his or her life, attempt to make bread. And remember, if at first you do not succeed, try, try again. Even today, I sometimes have bread that does not turn out exactly how I would have liked it to and that is ok. I simply start again.

FRIED DOUGH
MASSA FRITTA

INGREDIENTS:

- 6 cups all-purpose flour
- 3 cups warm water
- 2 envelopes active dry yeast, or 2 teaspoons
- ½ teaspoon salt
- 2 cups vegetable oil

"For a fancier presentation, before you drop the dough into the oil, you can roll the pinches of dough on a lightly floured surface with a rolling pin into perfect circles. You can also sweeten these snacks by garnishing them with confectioners' sugar once they have cooled." – Elisa

DIRECTIONS:

In a small mixing bowl, add 1 cup of warm water, ½ cup of flour and the yeast and mix with a fork. Allow the mixture to sit for 30-40 minutes.

In a large mixing bowl or electric mixer, add 2 cups of warm water, 5½ cups of flour, salt, and the mixture from the small bowl. If you choose to use a mixing bowl, knead the dough by hand for 15 minutes. If you are using an electric mixture knead the dough for 10 minutes.

Cover the dough with a clean towel and set aside in a warm, non-drafty area for 1½-2 hours until the dough has tripled in size.

Heat the vegetable oil in a large skillet on high heat. The oil must be hot. Reduce the heat and prepare the dough.

Pinch pieces of dough to your liking and flatten between your hands and place in the skillet. Allow frying for 2-3 minutes and flipping with tongs to allow frying for an additional 2-3 minutes. Dough should achieve a golden color. Once you feel confident, drop 3-4 at a time into the skillet. Remove the fried dough from the oil and dry on a paper towel before serving. If you prefer, you can add a pinch of salt to the dough while they are in the skillet.

ZUCCHINI BREAD

"This recipe makes two bread loaves, one for you and one for a friend. An Old Italian superstition says that it is bad luck to make a single loaf of bread. You never know when you may have surprise visitors, and you never want to run out of food when you have guests at your table." – Elisa

INGREDIENTS:

- 3 eggs
- 3 cups all-purpose flour
- 1 cup vegetable oil
- 1¼ cup sugar
- 1 teaspoon salt
- 1 teaspoon cinnamon
- 1 teaspoon baking soda
- ½ teaspoon baking powder
- 1½ cups chopped walnuts
- 2 cups grated fresh zucchini

DIRECTIONS:

Preheat oven to 325 degrees F.

Using an electric mixer, beat the eggs and sugar. Add flour, oil, salt, baking soda, baking powder, and cinnamon and continue to mix for 5 minutes. Finally add walnuts and zucchini until blended evenly.

Grease 2 loaf pans and pour the batter evenly into the pans. Bake for 1 hour. Remove from oven, and carefully remove loaves from pans, freeing the edges with a knife. Place on wire racks to cool.

BREAKFAST SODA BREAD

INGREDIENTS:

- 2 eggs
- 4 cups all-purpose flour
- ¼ cup butter, melted
- 1¼ cup buttermilk
- 1 teaspoon salt
- 1 teaspoon baking powder
- 1 teaspoon baking soda
- 1 cup raisins
- 2 teaspoons cinnamon

DIRECTIONS:

Preheat oven to 350 degrees F.

In a mixing bowl sift flour, sugar, salt and baking powder. Add butter and raisins and mix well. In a separate bowl, whisk the eggs, buttermilk and baking soda. Add this mixture to the flour mixture and stir until it is moist and even. Grease an 8-inch iron frying pan, and pour in the mixture. Bake for 1 hour and 20 minutes. Remove from oven and serve hot and from the pan.

NUT BREAD
PANE CON NOCE

INGREDIENTS:

- 2¼ cups all-purpose flour
- ¾ cup sugar
- ¾ teaspoon salt
- 1 teaspoon baking soda
- 2 teaspoons baking powder
- 1 cup raisins
- ½ cup walnuts, chopped
- 1 cup orange juice
- 1 egg, beaten
- 2 teaspoons butter, melted
- 1 teaspoon vanilla extract
- 1 teaspoon orange extract

DIRECTIONS:

Preheat oven to 350 degrees F.

In a large mixing bowl, combine the sugar, raisins, orange juice, egg, butter, vanilla and orange extracts. In a separate bowl, sift the flour, salt, baking soda, and baking powder. Add the flour mixture to the juice mixture and blend thoroughly. Stir in the walnuts. Pour the mixture in a greased loaf pan. Bake for 45 minutes. Remove from oven, then gently remove from the pan and cool on a wire rack.

ITALIAN STYLE BAGELS
TARALLI

- 6 eggs
- 1¼ cup all-purpose flour
- ½ teaspoon baking powder
- ¼ cup olive oil

OPTIONAL ICING:

- 2 cups confectioners' sugar
- ¾ cup ice water

DIRECTIONS

Preheat oven to 475 degrees F.

Boil a large saucepan full of water. With an electric mixer, add the eggs and beat. Then add the flour, baking powder and oil and knead well.

Bring the dough to a floured surface and knead by hand for another 5 minutes. Roll the dough into an 8-inch circle and ½ inch thick. Take the ends of the stick and form a circle. Set aside on a floured surface.

One by one drop the rings of Taralli into the boiling water. They will sink to the bottom; so try not to have more than 8 in the pot at a time. Using a wooden spoon stir occasionally to keep them from sticking to the bottom of the pot. As they float to the top, remove and dry on a clean towel or cloth.

Take each Tarallo and with a sharp blade make an incision of about ¼ of an inch on the outside edge of the Tarallo. Then place the cut Taralli on a flat oven grill rack and bake them for 7 minutes. Lower the temperature to 420 degrees F and continue baking them for an additional 30 minutes until they turn lightly golden.

While the Taralli are baking, prepare the icing by melting the water and sugar in a pot over the stove, stirring and letting the water boil. Once the water boils, continue stirring and let simmer for 5 minutes.

Once the Taralli are finished baking, remove from the oven and place on wire rack. Let them cool for about 15 minutes and pour the icing over the tops. Place some waxed paper under the wire racks to avoid a mess. Let the icing settle and harden, then serve.

EASTER BREAD

PANE DI PASQUA

INGREDIENTS

- 4 eggs
- 2 envelopes active dry yeast, or 2 teaspoons
- 5 cups all-purpose flour
- ½ cup warm water
- 1 cup sugar
- 1 cup whole milk
- ½ cup vegetable oil

DIRECTIONS

Preheat oven to 325 degrees F.

In a small bowl, mix warm water, 1 tablespoon of flour, and yeast and allow to sit in a warm place for 30 minutes.

On a clean wooden or marble-like surface make a mound of the flour, hollow out the center with a spoon. Add the eggs to the well, and whisk with a fork. Add the sugar, milk, oil, and yeast mixture and continue to whisk with a fork, gradually adding the mound of flour. Once you have incorporated all the flour, knead well until the dough has an even consistency.

Place the dough in a bowl at least 3 times the size of the dough ball and set aside in a warm place covered with a cloth to rise for 2-3 hours. Once the dough has risen, choose the shape and form you want for your loaves. You can use 2 traditional bread loaf pans, 2 9-inch cake pans, tube pans, or braid the dough into a ring and place on a cookie sheet. Whichever form you choose, lightly grease the pans or cookie sheet. Garnish with colorful sprinkles.

Bake for 50 minutes to 1 hour. Remove from pan carefully, and cool loaves on a wire rack.

HAM & CHEESE STROMBOLI

STROMBOLI CON FORMAGGIO E PROSCIUTTO COTTO

INGREDIENTS:

- 1 envelope active dry yeast, or 1 teaspoon
- 5 cups all-purpose flour
- 2½ cups warm water
- Pinch of salt
- ¼ cup olive oil
- 1 egg
- 2 pounds sliced deli ham
- ½ pound salami or pepperoni
- 2 pounds fresh mozzarella, sliced

DIRECTIONS:

In a small bowl, mix ½ cup warm water, ½ cup flour, and yeast and allow to sit in a warm place for 30 minutes. On a clean wooden or marble-like surface, make a mound of the flour. Hollow out the center with a spoon. Add the remaining water to the well, and whisk with a fork. Add the oil, salt, and yeast mixture, and continue to whisk with a fork, gradually adding the flour from the mound. Once you have incorporated all the flour, knead well until the dough has an even consistency. Place the dough in an olive oil greased bowl at least 3 times the size of the dough ball. Brush some olive oil on top of the dough and set aside covered with a cloth in a warm place to rise for 2-3 hours.

Once the dough has risen, separate the dough into 2 equal portions. Roll out each portion separately into a rectangular shape on a lightly floured surface. Divide the ham, cheese, and salami or pepperoni into two parts. Line the surface of the dough with a layer of ham, then cheese and then salami or pepperoni. Roll the dough lengthwise, tightly. Repeat with the second half and place the rolled Stromboli on a greased cookie sheet. Seal the end of the roll by brushing with a beaten egg. Allow to rest on the pan for 10-15 minutes before placing in oven.

Preheat oven to 350 degrees F. Place in the oven and bake for 30 minutes. Remove and allow to cool for 20 minutes. Slice into 1½-2 inch slices and serve.

HAM & CHEESE STROMBOLI

STROMBOLI CON FORMAGGIO E PROSCIUTTO COTTO

PEPPERS & EGG STROMBOLI

STROMBOLI CON PEPERONI E UOVA

INGREDIENTS

- 1 envelope active dry yeast, or 1 teaspoon
- 5 cups all-purpose flour
- 2½ cups warm water
- Pinch of salt
- ½ cup olive oil
- 4 red peppers, chopped
- 1 medium onion, chopped
- 5 eggs
- 1 pound fresh mozzarella, sliced
- ¼ cup fresh Parmesan cheese, grated

DIRECTIONS

In a small bowl, mix ½ cup warm water, ½ cup flour, and yeast and allow to sit in a warm place for 30 minutes. On a clean wooden or marble-like surface, make a mound of the flour. Hollow out the center with a spoon. Add the remaining water to the well, and whisk with a fork. Add ¼ cup of oil, salt, and yeast mixture, and continue to whisk with a fork, gradually adding the flour from the mound. Once you have incorporated all the flour, knead well until the dough has an even consistency. Place the dough in an olive oil greased bowl at least 3 times the size of the dough ball. Brush some olive oil on top of the dough and set aside covered with a cloth in a warm place to rise for 2-3 hours.

While the dough is rising, heat the remaining olive oil in a sauté pan over medium heat. Add the peppers and onion and sauté until the peppers are tender. Beat 4 eggs and add them to the sauté pan and blend for 3-4 minutes. Add the Parmesan cheese and remove from heat.

Preheat oven to 350 degrees F.

Once the dough has risen, separate the dough into 2 equal portions. Roll out each portion separately into a rectangular shape on a lightly floured surface. Divide the mixture into two parts. Spread the pepper mixture over the surface of the dough. Spread the mozzarella cheese over the mixture. Roll the dough lengthwise, tightly. Repeat with the second half and place the rolled Stromboli on a greased cookie sheet. Seal the end of the roll by brushing with a beaten egg. Allow to rest on the pan for 10-15 minutes before placing in oven.

Place in the oven and bake for 30 minutes. Remove and allow to cool for 20 minutes. Slice in 1½ -2 inch slices and serve.

RUSTIC BREAD
PANE RUSTICO

INGREDIENTS

- 6½ cups all-purpose flour
- 2 envelopes active dry yeast, or 2 teaspoons
- 3 cups warm water
- ¼ cup of olive oil

DIRECTIONS

In a small bowl, mix 1 cup of warm water, ½ cup of flour, and yeast and allow to sit in a warm place for 30 minutes. On a clean wooden or marble-like surface make a mound with the remaining 6 cups of flour, hollow out the center with a spoon. Add the remaining 2 cups of water and the yeast mixture to the well, and whisk in the flour with a fork. Once you have incorporated all the flour, knead well until the dough has an even consistency. Place the dough in an olive oil greased bowl at least 3 times the size of the dough ball . Brush some olive oil on top of the dough and set aside covered with a cloth in a warm place to rise for 2-3 hours. Knead the dough again for 4-6 minutes and return to the bowl. Cover and allow to rise for an additional hour.

Once the dough has risen and doubled in size, preheat oven to 350 degrees F. Turn dough over onto a lightly floured surface and knead for 3-4 minutes. Roll the dough into an oval shape, approximately ¾ of the length of a cookie sheet. Place the dough on a greased cookie sheet and allow to rest on the pan for 10-15 minutes before placing in oven. Bake for 1 hour. For rolls, take a tennis ball amount of dough, and roll between the palms of your hands and place on the cookie sheet 2-inches apart. Remove from oven and cool on a wire rack.

CALZONE

INGREDIENTS

FOR THE DOUGH:

- 2½ cups all-purpose flour
- 1 teaspoon salt
- 1 envelope active dry yeast
- 1¼ cup warm water
- 2 tablespoons vegetable oil

FOR THE FILLING:

- 1 medium onion, chopped
- 1 garlic clove, minced
- ½ cup fresh mushrooms, chopped
- ½ cup prosciutto, chopped
- ½ cup salami, chopped
- ¾ cup fresh mozzarella cheese, shredded
- ¼ cup fresh parsley, finely chopped
- ½ teaspoon basil, crumbled
- 1 egg yolk
- Salt and fresh black pepper to taste
- 2 tablespoons olive oil

FOR THE GLAZE:

- 1 egg
- 1 tablespoon water

DIRECTIONS

In a small bowl, mix 1 cup of warm water, ½ cup of flour, and yeast and allow to sit in a warm place for 30 minutes. Add the vegetable oil, salt, the remaining flour and mix. Turn the dough onto a lightly floured wooden or marble-like surface and knead until smooth and elastic. You can also use an electric mixer with a kneading attachment.

Lightly grease a medium-sized bowl. Place the dough in the bowl and rotate to grease the surface evenly. Cover with a kitchen towel and place in a warm, draft-free area, and allow to rise until doubled in size, or approximately 2 hours.

While the dough is rising, you can prepare your filling. Heat the olive oil in a medium-sized skillet over medium heat. Add the onion, garlic, mushrooms and sauté for 5 minutes. Remove from the heat and allow to cool to room temperature. Add the meats, cheese, parsley, basil, egg yolk, and salt and pepper; mix well and set aside.

Once the dough has risen, separate the dough into 2 equal portions. Roll out each portion separately into a circular shape on a lightly-floured surface. Divide the filling into two parts. Line the center of the dough with the filling on each portion of dough. Fold the dough, and press down tightly on the ends. Seal the ends by brushing them with the glaze. Place on a greased cookie sheet. Allow to rest on the pan for 10-15 minutes before placing in oven.

Preheat oven to 350 degrees F.

Place in the oven and bake for 30 minutes. Remove and allow to cool for 20 minutes.

MARGARITA PIZZA

PIZZA ALLA MARGHERITA

MAKES 4 PIZZAS

INGREDIENTS:

FOR THE DOUGH:

- 1 envelope active dry yeast
- 1 ¼ cup warm water
- 2 tablespoons olive oil
- 1 teaspoon salt
- 4 cups all-purpose flour

FOR THE TOPPING:

- 2 cups marinara sauce, see my recipe in sauces, pg. 126
- 1 teaspoon salt
- Pinch fresh black pepper
- ½ teaspoon oregano
- 1 pound fresh Mozzarella cheese, shredded

DIRECTIONS:

In a medium, glass mixing bowl, dissolve the yeast in warm water; stir in the oil and salt. Mix in the flour and blend thoroughly. Turn over the dough on a lightly-floured wooden or marble-like surface and knead the dough until it is smooth and elastic, about 15 minutes. Brush the mixing bowl with oil and return the dough to the bowl and brush the dough with oil. Cover and place in a warm area to rise for 3 hours.

Preheat the oven to 400 degrees F.

Remove the dough from the bowl, knead lightly and divide into 4 equal parts. Roll each piece into a 9-inch diameter. Place the rolled out dough onto greased pizza pans or cookie sheets. Dent here and there and turn up edges. Brush the dough again with some oil. Mix the marinara sauce with the salt, pepper, and oregano. Spread the sauce over the dough. Add the Mozzarella cheese and place in the oven for 15 minutes, or until the dough is golden and crisp. Remove from the pan and serve.

You can add more toppings if you like.

FOCACCIA BREAD

INGREDIENTS

- 5 cups all-purpose flour
- 2 cups warm water
- 1 envelope active dry yeast or 1 teaspoon
- 1 tablespoon oregano
- 2 tablespoons fresh rosemary
- 1 tablespoon black pepper
- 1 teaspoon garlic salt
- 1 teaspoon salt
- ¼ cup olive oil

DIRECTIONS

Mix the flour, water, and yeast together in a large glass bowl. Set aside in a warm non-drafty space and cover with a dishtowel. Allow to rise for 30-40 minutes.

Once the dough has risen, turn the dough over onto a floured surface and knead for 3-4 minutes. Add some flour if the dough is sticky. Place the dough in a bowl at least 2 times the size of the dough ball. Set aside covered with a cloth in a warm place to rise for an additional 15-20 minutes.

Preheat oven to 350 degrees F. Turn the dough over onto a floured surface and shape the dough into an oval shape, approximately ¾ of the length of a cookie sheet. Roll out the dough to an even thickness and poke the dough all over with your fingertips.

Grease the cookie sheet with some olive oil. Gently place the dough on the greased cookie sheet, and sprinkle the top with the remaining olive oil. Then top with fresh rosemary, salt, oregano, garlic salt, and black pepper and bake for 1 hour.

For rolls, take a tennis ball amount of dough and roll between the palms of your hands, and place on the greased cookie sheet 2 inches apart and bake for 1 hour.

Remove from oven and cool on a wire rack.

FOCACCIA & RUSTIC BREAD

PANE RUSTICO

SEE PAGE 45

TYPES OF PASTA

MANICOTTI

is a stuffed, baked, large, tube–shaped pasta about 6 inches long, and 1 inch in diameter. The dough is cut and filled with flavorful cheeses, then rolled, covered with sauce and baked in the oven.

LINGUINE

is a narrow, flat version of round spaghetti. I use this type of pasta with seafood dishes. However it works with almost any type of pasta sauce.

PAPPARDELLE

is a rustic, pre–pasta machine type of pasta noodle. After rolling the pasta dough by hand, using a knife or rolling cutter, you cut 3–inch long by 1½–inch wide strips. I serve this type of pasta with meat–based sauces.

PENNE, RIGATONI, & ZITI

are common short pasta shapes. I must admit, I do not make my own, but many modern electric pasta machines allow you to do so. I use Penne and Ziti for all types of sauces. But I reserve Rigatoni for my pasta al forno (baked pasta).

FETTUCCINE

is very similar to Linguine, but wider by ¼ inch. It is usually the widest–cut attachment of the pasta machine. I reserve this type of pasta for my blush and cream–based sauce.

RAVIOLI

is pasta dough folded to create pillow–shaped pasta stuffed with a variety of cheeses, meat, seafood or vegetable fillings. I am a traditionalist and stay true to their original stuffing of ricotta and spinach. They can be served with butter, olive oil, sugar, sauce, or in soups.

SPAGHETTI

is the most famous type of pasta. It is said to be the oldest shape known. And as much as it may hurt some Italians feelings, we must credit this type of pasta to the Chinese, brought back by Marco Polo in the 13th century. Spaghetti is long, thin, and round, and the thickness of spaghetti varies from region to region. I use the traditional 'chitarra' or my manual pasta machine. It is best paired with oil– or tomato– based sauces.

TAGLIATELLE

is another rustic and classic thin egg noodle of traditional Italian cooking. They are similar in thickness to Pappardelle, but resemble fettuccine. To prepare them, roll out the fresh egg pasta into 10–inch long strips by 4 inches wide. Roll them tight and then using a sharp knife, slice the roll into ½–inch wide slices. This pasta is thick and wide enough to hold heavy sauces.

POLENTA

is a cornmeal–based substitute to egg and flour–based pasta. Historically, polenta was considered a peasant's meal and more sophisticated Italians would not lower themselves to eat it. Little did they know, many Italian families like mine did not mind this alternative, especially when topped with our freshly made sausage, sauce and homemade cheeses.

SCRIPPELLE

have a story of their own!

FRESH EGG PASTA DOUGH

SERVES 4–6 PEOPLE

INGREDIENTS

- 6 jumbo size eggs
- 3½ cups all-purpose flour
- Olive oil

DIRECTIONS

To mix the dough by hand:

Mound the flour in the center of a clean large wooden or flat surface. Make a well in the center of the flour and add the eggs. Using a fork, beat the eggs together. Then begin to incorporate the flour, starting with the inner rim of the well. As you expand the well, keep pushing the flour up to retain the well shape. (Do not worry if it looks messy.)

When half of the flour is incorporated, the dough will begin to come together. Start kneading the dough, using primarily the palms of your hands. Once the dough is a cohesive shape, set the dough aside and scrape up and discard any dried bits of dough.

Continue kneading for 10 minutes, dusting the board with additional flour as necessary. The dough should be elastic and a little sticky. Put dough in a bowl, spread olive oil around dough mass, cover, and allow to rest for 30 minutes at room temperature before using.

To mix the dough in an electric mixer:

If you have a dough hook for a mixer, mix until dough forms into a mass. Remove and follow steps from above. Add to bowl, spread olive oil around dough mass, and allow to rest at room temperature. After resting the dough, knead again for an additional 10 minutes. Always keep your dough covered when not in use.

DIRECTIONS

To roll the dough out by hand:

FOR RAVIOLI, LASAGNA, CANNELLONI, PAPPARDELLE, MANICOTTI, AND TAGLIATELLE

After 30 minutes have passed, cut the ball of dough into four equal pieces. Cover and reserve the pieces you are not immediately using to prevent them from drying out. Dust your surface and dough with a little flour and roll out the dough with a rolling pin into a rectangular shape, by rolling lengthwise, then widthwise. Cover until you are ready to use. For cutting or filling follow the next steps under each type of pasta recipe.

FOR SPAGHETTI AL LA CHITARRA

Press the sheet of dough through the wire rack, dust with some flour and cover until ready to use.

To roll the dough out using a manual pasta machine:

FOR RAVIOLI, LASAGNA, CANNELLONI, PAPPARDELLE, MANICOTTI, AND TAGLIATELLE

After resting the mass for 30 minutes, cut the ball of dough it into four equal pieces. Cover and reserve the pieces you are not immediately using to prevent them from drying out. Dust your surface and dough with a little flour and press the dough into a rectangle. Roll through the widest setting on the pasta machine.

Fold this rectangle of dough like a letter, and roll through again. Repeat the rolling and folding a few more times, to knead and smooth the dough. Repeat with the remaining pieces of dough. Switch to the next-narrower setting on the machine. Roll a dough strip through, short end first. Repeat with remaining dough strips. Continue this process with narrower settings, now rolling only once through each setting, until you've gotten to the next-to-last setting and the dough strips are about as wide as the machine (6 inches).

Your final dough strips should be paper-thin, about ⅛-inch thick. Dust the sheets of dough with flour as needed.

Note: If you are preparing Lasagna, you will need to triple the recipe for a 13-inch by 9-inch by 2-inch casserole pan of Lasagna.

FOR SPAGHETTI, LINGUINE, AND FETTUCCINI

After resting the mass for 30 minutes, cut the ball of dough into roughly 1-inch slices. Cover and reserve the pieces you are not immediately using to prevent them from drying out. Dust your surface and dough with a little flour and press dough into a rectangle, then put into pasta machine to flatten about 3-4 times, then select pasta you want to make. Most hand machines have Spaghetti and Fettuccini or Linguine settings.

Notes: If you are using an electric mixer attachment or electric pasta machine, you can skip this step and follow the instructions of your device and select your desired pasta type, including spaghetti, linguine, fettuccini, penne, ziti, and rigatoni. As you finish rolling your pasta or feeding it through your electric machines, place on a floured surface and cover.

PENNE WITH CREAM SAUCE

PENNE ALLA PANNA E PANCETTA

SERVES 6 PEOPLE

INGREDIENTS:

- 1 pound pancetta or bacon, cubed
- 1 stick butter
- 2 tablespoons all-purpose flour
- 2 pints heavy cream
- 1 cup fresh Pecorino Romano or Parmesan cheese, grated
- 1 pound box penne pasta

DIRECTIONS:

In a medium saucepan, melt the butter over medium heat. Add in the flour and mix well. Sauté the pancetta for 4-5 minutes, or fry the bacon until cooked. Drain any oil from the pan and add the meat to the butter. Add the heavy cream and cheese and continue to cook over low heat, stirring occasionally.

While you are preparing the sauce, bring a large stockpot of water to a boil. Once boiling, drop in the pasta and cook according to the box instructions. Drain pasta and transfer to a serving bowl. Pour in cream sauce and toss gently. Garnish with more grated cheese and serve.

ZITI WITH LENTILS

PASTA E LENTICCHIE

SERVES 6 PEOPLE

INGREDIENTS

- 1½ cups dry lentils (or canned, drained, and rinsed)
- ¼ cup olive oil
- 4 ounces pancetta, chopped into ¼-inch squares
- 2 medium onions, chopped
- 1 clove garlic, chopped
- ¼ cup fresh parsley, chopped, including the stems
- Salt and fresh ground black pepper, to taste
- ½ cup fresh Pecorino Romano or Parmesan cheese, grated
- 1 pound dry ziti pasta

DIRECTIONS

Fill a medium saucepan halfway with water and add a pinch of salt; bringing the water to a rapid boil. Once boiling, add the lentils and continue to cook for 30 minutes, stirring occasionally until the lentils are tender. Drain the lentils and set aside. If you are using canned lentils, you do not have to boil them; simply drain and rinse them under cold water.

Using a large stockpot, boil water for pasta and cook al dente according to the package instructions.

While your pasta water is coming to a boil, heat the olive oil in a medium sauté pan over medium-high heat. Add the pancetta, onions, parsley and garlic; sauté and stir continuously for 5 minutes. Add the lentils and continue to sauté for 5 minutes. Add salt and pepper to taste.

Transfer a ladle full of pasta water into the lentils and pancetta and allow to cream for a few minutes. Transfer the pasta to a serving bowl and gradually mix in the lentils and pancetta. Garnish with the cheese and some more fresh parsley leaves and serve hot.

POTATO GNOCCHI

GNOCCHI DI PATATE

SERVES 8 PEOPLE

INGREDIENTS:

- 5 pounds Idaho potatoes, washed
- 4 eggs
- 4 cups all-purpose flour
- ¼ cup olive oil
- 1 tablespoon salt
- ½ cup Fresh Pecorino Romano or Parmesan cheese, grated
- Tomato or cream sauce of choice

DIRECTIONS:

Place the potatoes in a large stockpot and fill pot ¾ of the way with water. Place the pot over medium-high heat and boil the potatoes until tender or approximately 30 minutes. Drain and let the potatoes sit until cool enough to peel. Prepare the sauce of your choice.

Pass the potatoes through a potato ricer or grate them on the large holes of a box grater. This should produce approximately 8 cups of grated potatoes. On a wooden or marble-like surface, make a mound with flour and spoon out a well in the middle. Add the eggs to the well and beat the eggs with a fork. Mix in the potatoes, oil, and salt with the eggs and begin to fold in the flour. Once you have mixed in enough flour to soak the eggs, begin to fold in the remaining flour with your hands and form dough. If the mixture is too dry, add a little water. The dough should give under slight pressure.

Lightly flour the surface, and cut the dough into 6 pieces. Roll each piece into a rope about ½-inch in diameter. Cut diagonally into 1-inch-long pieces. Lightly flour the gnocchi as you cut them. Place the cut gnocchi on floured baking sheets. If you are not using the gnocchi immediately, refrigerate them for use later that day or freeze them for future use.

When ready to cook, bring a large pot of water to a boil and add a pinch of salt. Drop in the gnocchi and cook. Once they begin to rise to the surface, wait one minute, remove the cooked gnocchi with a skimmer, and place in a serving bowl. Spoon and fold in the sauce and garnish with the grated cheese. Serve immediately.

" This is the favorite dish of my grandsons Bobby and Sean. So I always have some gnocchi frozen and ready to cook just in case they pay me a visit" – Elisa

TIMBALLO

SERVING DEPENDS ON SIZE OF PAN BUT GENERALLY 10-12 PEOPLE.

INGREDIENTS:

- 2 pounds fresh mozzarella cheese, shredded
- 1 cup fresh Pecorino Romano cheese, grated
- 2 eggs
- 2-3 portions fresh scrippelles, see my recipe, pg.64
- ¼ cup milk
- 1 stick salted butter, cut into small cubes
- 2 pounds mini meatballs, see my recipe under Meats, pg.146
- Fresh tomato marinara sauce, see my recipe under Sauces, pg.126

"You can simplify this recipe by preparing the timbalo in a greased 13 x 9 x 2-inch glass casserole dish." - Elisa

DIRECTIONS:

Prepare a pot of my fresh tomato marinara sauce, mini meatballs, and scrippelle.

Preheat oven to 350 degrees F. Beat the eggs and milk in a small bowl. Use an extra large deep round cake pan, 13-15 inches in diameter. Line the pan with waxed paper, allowing for the paper to overlap the pan by 2 inches all around.

Line the bottom of the pan with scrippelle, overlapping to cover the entire surface. You can have the ends turn up on the side of the pan. Brush the scrippelle with the egg mixture, then ladle some sauce evenly over the scrippelle. Add a generous amount of mini meatballs, mozzarella, butter cubes, and Pecorino cheese. Add another layer of scrippelle and repeat the process. Once you reach the top of the pan, tuck the top layer of scrippelle down the sides and add a ladle of sauce and grated cheese over the top. Place in the oven and cook for 90 minutes. Remove the timballo from the oven and allow to cool for 5-10 minutes. Place a plate as large in diameter as the pan over the top and flip the timballo over. Lift the pan gently and peel away the wax paper. Bring to the table and serve. Allow your guests to see how beautiful your timballo is, then slice like a pie or cut into squares.

TIMBALLO

CLASSIC CANNELLONI

SERVES 4 – 6 PEOPLE

INGREDIENTS

- 1 portion of my fresh egg pasta dough, see my recipe in Pastas pg.52

FOR THE FILLING:

- 1½ pounds fresh ground beef or pork
- 1 large onion, finely chopped
- 2 cups fresh spinach, finely chopped
- 2 carrots, peeled and finely chopped
- 2 celery stalks, finely chopped
- ¼ cup fresh parsley, chopped, including the stem
- 1 garlic clove, whole
- ¼ cup fresh oregano, chopped
- ½ cup fresh Pecorino Romano cheese, grated
- ½ cup fresh Parmesan cheese, grated
- ½ cup extra-virgin olive oil
- 1 cup chicken stock
- 1 cup dry white wine
- 28-ounce can crushed tomatoes
- Salt to taste

FOR THE BESCIAMELLA SAUCE:

- 4 cups whole milk
- 1 stick salted butter
- 2 tablespoons all-purpose flour
- ¼ cup fresh Parmesan cheese, grated
- ¼ cup fresh Pecorino Romano cheese, grated

DIRECTIONS

Prepare a large stockpot of water with a pinch of salt and bring to a boil for the pasta.

Prepare the filling:

In a large skillet, heat ¼ cup olive oil over medium heat. Add the onion and sauté for 3-5 minutes. Add the ground meat and wine and continue to sauté for 10 to 15 minutes, breaking down the meat with spatula into the smallest pieces possible. In a medium saucepan, heat the other ¼ cup of olive oil and garlic over medium heat and simmer for 2-3 minutes, then add the crushed tomatoes and ¼ cup of water and simmer until ready to use.

Add the chicken stock, carrots, celery, parsley, oregano, and a pinch of salt and rosemary. Pour in the hot chicken stock, and simmer for 10 minutes until the vegetables are soft. Finally, add the spinach and 1 cup of the tomato sauce and sauté for an additional 5 minutes. Remove from the heat and set aside.

Prepare the Besciamella Sauce:

Melt the butter in a small saucepan. When melted, stir in the flour to make a smooth paste. Cook, stirring with a wooden spoon for 2-3 minutes. Pour in the milk, whisking to avoid lumps. Bring to a simmer, whisking until thickened (approximately 5 minutes). Remove from heat, and whisk in grated cheese.

Prepare your Pasta:

From the hand-rolled or machine-pressed fresh egg pasta dough you prepared, cut 4-inch by 6-inch rectangular strips of dough. Your water should be boiling by now, so drop 3-4 strips of dough into the boiling water at a time and remove with a handheld strainer when they rise to the top. Dip in a bowl of cold water. Arrange the cooked pasta on a cloth towel and allow to cool.

Preheat oven to 400 degrees F.

Fill the Cannelloni:

Spread 1 cup of the Besciamella sauce in the bottom of a 13 x 9 x 2-inch glass casserole dish. Add 3 tablespoons of the tomato sauce and spread thoroughly over the pan base. Spread about ½ cup of the filling along one side of the dough strip lengthwise; roll up and fit them closely together in the baking dish. Spread the remaining Besciamella over the top of the cannelloni and add the remaining tomato sauce.

Garnish with grated cheeses. Cover the casserole dish with aluminum foil and bake until heated through, about 10-15 minutes. Uncover and bake until browned and bubbly, an additional 10-15 minutes. Remove from the oven and serve.

ORIGIN OF THE SCRIPPELLE

Today you will find this treasure of the Italian kitchen throughout Abruzzo, but it originated in Teramo, and still remains a characteristic feature in kitchens all over Teramo. Legend tells us that French Soldiers brought these crêpes across the Alps as an efficient way to feed their armies during the French occupation of the region around 1798. All they needed were some eggs and flour, and chickens were plentiful along the countryside. However, the idea of using them in soup is believed to have started when a cook named Enrico dei Castorano, forced to cook for the French soldiers, dropped some crêpes in a pot of broth by mistake, and in a panic served the dish as a soup, and "Scrippelle Mbusse" was born. True natives of Teramo and the surrounding area refute this idea and insist it had nothing to do with the French.

In fact, however scrippelle differ from crêpes in the preparation, ingredients and the use made of them in Teramo cuisine. In fact they have become an essential element for preparing savory dishes, although my granddaughter Lily loves them for breakfast. While I was visiting my son and his family during their work assignment in Shanghai, I taught their housemaid, Mei Lin how to prepare them. She then decided to prepare them for breakfast and fill them with Nutella. What child wouldn't fall in love with this treat!

Scrippelle are the key ingredient for several Teramana dishes including:

- **"SCRIPPELLE MBUSSE,"**
  are immersed in a light chicken broth after being sprinkled
  with Parmesan or Pecorino cheese, seasoned and rolled. (See my recipe in soups)

- **"TIMBALLO SCRIPPELLE,"**
  where they replace dough with crêpes
  in separating the layers of ingredients in a lasagna.

- **"SCRIPPELLE AL FORNO,"**
  where they are stuffed and cooked in the oven in a manner similar to cannelloni.

SCRIPPELLE

PASTA CRÊPES
SCRIPPELLE

MAKES ABOUT 26-30 CREPES

INGREDIENTS:

- 10 jumbo eggs
- 2½ cups all-purpose flour
- 3½ cups water
- 1 cup olive oil

DIRECTIONS:

Beat the eggs in an electric mixer, gradually sifting in the flour. Continue to beat at a very low speed for 5-10 minutes, while gradually adding the water. Continue to beat until the batter is very smooth, with no visible lumps.

Heat an 8- or 10-inch Teflon pan on low heat. You must use a Teflon pan to keep the crêpes from burning and sticking to the pan. I use an 8-inch pan, which normally yields 40-45 crêpes; a 10-inch pan will yield, 25-30.

Dip a paper towel into the cup of olive oil and grease the pan; you will need to repeat the greasing of the pan after every 3-4 crêpes. Using a ladle, spread the batter lightly to cover the entire diameter of the pan. Allow the crepe to cook for 2-3 minutes and remove with a fork and transfer to a paper towel-covered surface. Add some water if mixture is too thick and does not run easily through pan.

SCRIPPELLE LASAGNA IN WHITE SAUCE

SCRIPPELLE LASAGNA CON SALSA BIANCA

INGREDIENTS:

- 3 portions scrippelle crêpes
- 1 pound lean ground beef
- 1 small onion, chopped
- 6 cups chicken broth
- 2 pounds fresh mozzarella, shredded
- ½ cup fresh Parmesan cheese, grated
- 2 eggs
- ½ cup whole milk
- 1 stick salted butter, cut into small cubes
- Pinch of salt and fresh black pepper
- ¼ cup olive oil

DIRECTIONS:

Preheat oven to 350 degrees F.

Prepare the Filling:

In a medium sauté pan, heat the olive oil over medium heat and sauté the onion and garlic until the onions are soft. Add the ground meat, salt, pepper, and continue to sauté until the meat is brown. Drain the oil and set the meat aside. In a separate bowl beat the eggs and milk.

Assembling the Lasagna:

Add a layer of crêpes to the base of a 13 x 9 x 2-inch glass casserole pan, overlapping them slightly. Brush the sheets with the egg mixture. Sprinkle some ground meat, and top with some mozzarella and Parmesan cheese. Pour a layer of chicken broth over the crêpes and sprinkle some cubes of butter. Repeat this process until you have reached the top layer. Use any extra crêpes for soup on another occasion, as they are easy to freeze. The top layer should have a healthy portion of broth and grated cheese. Bake for 60-90 minutes covered. Most of the liquid should have evaporated. Remove from the oven and allow to sit for 20 minutes before serving.

" This is my son's favorite Lasagna-type dish,
so I make everyone else a red Lasagna,
and I make him his own. Because that is what Italian
mothers do for their sons." – Elisa

BAKED SCRIPPELLE

SCRIPPELLE AL FORNO

SERVES 4-6 PEOPLE

"This dish is the Abruzzese version
of classic Cannelloni and features
a cream-based sauce rather than tomato.
It also resembles my Lasagna Bianca
in taste but Scrippelle Mousse in presentation."
– Elisa

INGREDIENTS:

- 1 serving Besciamella sauce, see pg.129
- 1 portion Scrippelle crêpes, see pg.64
- 2 pounds ground beef or turkey
- 1 large onion, chopped
- ½ cup of fresh parsley, chopped, including the stem
- 1 celery stalk, chopped
- 1 carrot, peeled and chopped
- Salt and fresh black pepper to taste
- 2-3 tablespoons olive oil
- 1 cup fresh mozzarella cheese, shredded
- ¼ cup fresh Parmesan cheese, grated

BAKED SCRIPPELLE

SCRIPPELLE AL FORNO

DIRECTIONS:

Preheat oven to 350 degrees F.

Heat the olive oil in a large skillet over medium heat. Add the onion, parsley, carrot, and celery and sauté until soft. Add the ground meat and continue to sauté until the meat is lightly browned. Remove from heat and drain any grease from the pan.

Layer 2 Scrippelle on top of each other and spoon 1½–2 tablespoons of the meat mixture along one side. Add a heavy sprinkle of the mozzarella cheese. Roll the Scrippelle to secure the mixture and tuck the ends under. Line the finished Scrippelles in a glass 13 x 9 x 2-inch casserole pan. Cover the bottom of the pan with some sauce. Once you have filled the pan with rolled Scrippelle, pour the Besciamella sauce over the crepes and garnish with the grated cheese.

Place in the oven and bake for 30-40 minutes. If the sauce begins to harden and thicken, add some water. Remove from the oven and serve.

RAVIOLI WITH SUGAR

RAVIOLI DOLCI

SERVES 4–6 PEOPLE

INGREDIENTS

- 1 portion of my fresh egg pasta dough, see my recipe in Pastas, pg.52
- 1½ pound Ricotta Cheese, drained
- 1 egg
- ¼ cup sugar
- ½ teaspoon cinnamon
- 1 cup fresh Pecorino Romano cheese, shredded

DIRECTIONS

Fill a large stockpot with a pinch of salt and bring to a boil to cook the Ravioli.

In a glass bowl, beat the egg and add the ricotta, sugar and cinnamon and mix thoroughly. Spread the strips of pasta dough on a clean surface dusted with flour. Starting 3 inches from one end, drop a tablespoon of the mixture in the center of the dough, and continue to drop every 3 inches. Fold over the pasta dough and press down on the ends where the pasta dough meets. Using a wheel cutter, cut the ravioli into moon shapes with the lump of ricotta centered on each cut. Drop 6-8 ravioli at a time into the boiling water for 5–7 minutes, and scoop out with a ladle and transfer to serving dish or plates.

Serve with my traditional tomato sauce recipe or simply melt 2 cups of butter in a small saucepan and pour over the ravioli and garnish with the Pecorino Romano Cheese.

"Ravioli with Sugar is a classic dish of Abruzzo cuisine traditionally served during Carnevale, just before the Lenten Season begins. This was a favorite of my late sister-in-law Pierina. She and I were best friends from the age of 2 and we became sisters when she married my brother Joe." - Elisa

In Loving Memory of Pierina Pizii Fantozzi
July 23, 1939 - January 13, 2013

SPAGHETTI ALLA CHITARRA

INGREDIENTS:

FOR THE PASTA:

- 3½ cups all-purpose flour
- 6 eggs
- 1 pinch of salt

FOR THE SAUCE:

- ½ pound ground lamb
- ½ pound lean ground pork
- 4-6 beef ribs
- 4 28-ounce cans crushed tomatoes
- 3 cloves garlic, quartered
- ¼ cup butter
- 1 cup olive oil
- ½ cup fresh parsley, chopped, including the stems
- 1 large onion, sliced in half
- 1 carrot, grated
- 2 teaspoons salt
- 1 cup Fresh Pecorino Romano or Parmesan cheese, grated

DIRECTIONS:

Prepare the Pasta

Create a mound of flour on a clean surface and scoop out a hole in the center. Add the eggs to the center with a pinch of salt and beat the eggs into the flour with a fork until the two have formed a solid mixture. Knead into a satiny ball of dough. Flatten the dough about ½ inch thick with a rolling pin dusted with flour. Using your Chitarra, pass sheets of flattened dough through the wooden frame; if you do not have one, use a more modern pasta machine.

Prepare the Sauce

In a medium-sized saucepan, heat the olive oil and garlic for 5 minutes on low heat. Raise the heat to medium, and add the ground meats. Sauté for 3-4 minutes, then add the carrots, onions, butter and salt; sauté for an additional 3-4 minutes. Finally add crushed tomatoes, 1 cup of water, ribs and parsley. Stirring occasionally, cook uncovered for at least 1-1½ hours. Remove the ribs and onion right before you are ready to use the sauce and set aside. Fill a large stockpot with water and add a pinch of salt. Heat on high until the water boils and drop in the spaghetti, cooking for 2-3 minutes or until it rises to the surface. Drain the pasta and transfer to a serving bowl. Add the sauce and half of the cheese and mix. Garnish with the remaining ½ cup of cheese and ribs, then serve.

"I first learned how to make homemade pasta as a young girl by using this instrument of the Italian Kitchen called a 'Chitarra'. It is a wooden frame with steel wires strung across in straight lines and resembles a harp. It produces thick square spaghetti. This sauce calls for 3 kinds of meat and was used only for holidays and special celebrations in my family." – Elisa

LINGUINE WITH CLAMS

LINGUINE CON VONGOLE

SERVES 4-6 PEOPLE

INGREDIENTS

- 2½ pounds small clams, scrubbed
- 4 garlic cloves, finely chopped
- ½ cup fresh parsley, chopped, including the stem
- ¼ cup crushed red pepper flakes
- 1 cup olive oil
- 1½ cup dry white wine
- 1 teaspoon salt
- ¼ cup salted butter
- Fresh black pepper to taste
- Fresh Parmesan cheese, grated
- 1 portion fresh egg linguine, see my recipe in Pastas, pg.52 or 1 pound of box pasta

DIRECTIONS

Prepare a large stockpot of water with a pinch of salt and bring to a boil for the pasta. Wash and scrub the clams under cold water and dry on a paper towel.

In a large sauté pan over medium-high, heat the oil and cook the garlic until it is lightly golden in color. Add the clams and pour wine over them. Season with salt and parsley. Cover and allow to simmer for 6-8 minutes until most the clams have opened. Discard any clams that fail to open.

As the pasta water begins to boil, drop in the fresh egg linguine you have prepared and cook for 3-5 minutes (If you are using dry pasta, cook according to box instructions.)

Drain the pasta and place in a large serving bowl. Remove the clams with a wire spoon and set aside in a bowl. Add the butter to the liquid in the sauté pan and whisk until liquid thickens. Pour the liquid over the pasta and toss well. Add the clams to the pasta and garnish with black pepper, parsley and a few pinches of cheese.

SPAGHETTI WITH GARLIC, OLIVE OIL AND HOT PEPPER

SPAGHETTI AGLIO, OLIO E PEPERONCINO

SERVES 4-6 PEOPLE

INGREDIENTS:

- 4 garlic cloves, chopped
- 1 tablespoon fresh parsley, chopped, including the stem
- ½ cup crushed red pepper flakes
- 1 cup olive oil
- 1 pinch and 1 teaspoon of salt
- Fresh Pecorino Romano cheese for garnish, grated
- 1 portion fresh egg spaghetti, see my recipe in Pastas, pg.52 or 1lb of box pasta

DIRECTIONS:

Fill a large stockpot with water and a pinch of salt and bring to a boil.

Once the water begins to boil, heat the olive oil in a medium sauté pan over medium heat, add the garlic and the red pepper flakes, and cook slowly until they turn golden.

While garlic is cooking, drop the fresh egg spaghetti you have prepared into boiling water and cook for 3-5 minutes (If you are using dry pasta, cook according to box instructions.) Drain the pasta and place in a serving bowl. Add the oil and parsley and toss thoroughly. Garnish with some cheese and serve immediately.

PENNE WITH ZUCCHINI

PENNE ALLE ZUCCHINE

INGREDIENTS:

- 2 pounds of fresh zucchini, peeled and thinly sliced
- 1 large onion, sliced
- 1 cup of olive oil
- ½ cup of Pecorino Romano cheese, shredded
- Salt and fresh black pepper to taste
- 1 pound of penne pasta

DIRECTIONS:

Fill a large stockpot with water and a pinch of salt and bring to a boil.

Heat the oil in a large sauté pan over medium heat. Add the onions and zucchini and sauté until tender, roughly 15 minutes. Add salt and pepper to taste; I recommend a pinch of each.

Cook your pasta and drain. Transfer the pasta to a serving bowl and add the onions and zucchini. Garnish with the shredded cheese and serve.

SPAGHETTI ALLA CARBONARA

SERVES 4–6 PEOPLE

INGREDIENTS

- ½ pound pancetta or bacon, cut into ½–inch pieces
- 3 eggs
- ¼ pound salted butter
- 1 cup fresh Pecorino Romano cheese, grated
- 1 teaspoon plus a pinch of salt
- 1 pinch of fresh black pepper
- ½ cup olive oil
- 1 portion fresh egg spaghetti, see my recipe in Pastas, Pg.52 or 1lb of box pasta

DIRECTIONS

Fill a large stockpot with water and a pinch of salt and bring to a boil.

Once water begins to boil, beat the eggs in a glass mixing bowl and add the cheese, teaspoon of salt, 1 pinch of pepper and blend well. In a medium–sized frying pan, heat the olive oil and fry the pancetta or bacon for 5 minutes. Do not drain the oil or grease.

While meat is cooking, drop in the fresh egg spaghetti you have prepared and cook for 3–5 minutes. (If you are using dry pasta, cook according to box instructions.)

Drain the pasta and place in a serving bowl. Add the meat and egg mixtures immediately and toss thoroughly. Garnish with more cheese and 1 pinch of pepper and serve immediately.

FETTUCCINE WITH PEAS AND HAM IN A CREAM SAUCE

FETTUCCINE CON PISELLI E PROSCIUTTO ALLA PANNA

SERVES 4–6 PEOPLE

INGREDIENTS

- ½ pound ham steak or pancetta, diced
- 1 medium onion, minced
- 2 cups frozen peas
- 1 cup chicken stock
- 1 cup heavy cream
- 2 tablespoons salted butter

- 1 pinch of salt
- 1 pinch of fresh ground black pepper
- 1 cup fresh Pecorino Romano cheese, grated
- 1 portion fresh egg fettuccine, see my recipe in Pastas, pg.52 or 1lb of box pasta

DIRECTIONS

Fill a large stockpot with water and a pinch of salt and bring to a boil. Place a large sauté pan over medium heat. Add and melt the butter; then add the onion and sauté approximately 10 minutes until golden and tender.

Add the peas and sauté for 5 minutes. Pour in the broth and bring to a soft boil and continue to sauté for 5 minutes. Add the ham and cream and bring to a soft boil.

While the sauce is cooking, drop in the fresh egg spaghetti you have prepared and cook for 3–5 minutes. (If you are using dry pasta, cook according to box instructions.)

Add the salt and pepper and the cheese to your sauce and mix thoroughly. Allow the cheese to dissolve and remove from heat.

Drain the pasta and place in a serving bowl. Add the sauce immediately and toss thoroughly. Garnish with more cheese and serve.

POLENTA WITH SAUSAGE SAUCE

POLENTA CON SUGO DI SALSICCIA

SERVES 6 PEOPLE

INGREDIENTS

FOR THE SAUCE:

- 3 pounds fresh Italian sausage
- 3 28-ounce cans crushed tomatoes
- 1 large onion, sliced in half
- 3 garlic cloves, sliced in half
- 1 basil leaf
- ¼ cup fresh parsley, chopped, including the stem
- ¼ cup olive oil
- Salt & fresh ground black pepper to taste

FOR THE POLENTA:

- 3 cups water
- 2 teaspoons salt
- 1 cup yellow Italian Polenta
- 1 cup fresh Pecorino Romano cheese for garnish, grated
- 2 teaspoons olive oil

DIRECTIONS

In a large stockpot, add the olive oil and set over medium high heat. Add the garlic, onion halves, and sausage and sauté for 5 minutes. Reduce the heat and add the crushed tomatoes, basil, parsley, and simmer at least one hour.

Bring the water to a boil in a large stockpot. Add 2 teaspoons of salt and gradually whisk in the polenta. Reduce the heat to low and cook until the mixture thickens and the polenta is tender but still very loose and creamy, stirring almost constantly for about 20-25 minutes. Turn off the heat. Add the olive oil and mix thoroughly. Remove the sausage from the sauce and slice roughly into ½-inch thick slices and set aside. Pour the polenta directly into individual bowls. Cover the entire surface of the polenta with the sauce and garnish with slices of the sausage and generous amounts of cheese.

POLENTA WITH SAUSAGE SAUCE

POLENTA CON SUGO DI SALSICCIA

PAPPARDELLE WITH WILD BOAR SAUCE

PAPPARDELLE CON RAGÙ DI CINGHIALE

SERVES 4-6 PEOPLE

INGREDIENTS:

FOR THE SAUCE:

- 2 pounds wild boar meat, cubed into 1-inch by 1-inch stew pieces
- 6 28-ounce cans crushed tomatoes
- 1 cup red wine
- 3 carrots, peeled and chopped
- 3 celery stalks, chopped
- 2 cups onions, chopped
- 2 tablespoons fresh rosemary
- 2 garlic cloves, chopped
- 2 bay leaves
- ½ cup olive oil
- Salt and fresh black pepper to taste

FOR THE PASTA:

- 1 portion fresh egg pasta strips, see my recipe in Pastas, pg.52
- Fresh Pecorino Romano cheese, grated

DIRECTIONS:

Prepare the Sauce:

Soak the boar pieces in a bath of cold water and a pinch of salt in a glass-mixing bowl in the refrigerator for 24 hours. Remove the boar from the refrigerator and rinse under cold water and place in a large sauté pan over medium heat. Sauté for 10-15 minutes. Drain the water that sweats from the meat.

In a large stockpot, heat the olive oil and garlic over medium heat for 3-5 minutes. Add the boar, carrots, celery, onions, rosemary, and bay leaf and sauté for another 10 minutes. Add the wine and 3-4 cups of water to cover the meat and simmer for 30 minutes. Maintain the level of liquid above the meat, by adding water when needed. After 30 minutes, add the tomatoes and a pinch of salt and black pepper and simmer on low heat for 1 to 1½ hours.

Prepare your Pasta:

20 minutes before your sauce is ready, prepare a large stockpot of water with a pinch of salt and bring to a boil.

From the hand-rolled or machine-pressed fresh egg pasta dough you prepared, cut 3-inch long by 1½-inch wide rectangular strips of dough with a knife or cutting wheel. The water should be boiling by now, so drop 3-4 strips of dough into the boiling water at a time and cook for 1-2 minutes and remove with a hand held strainer. Arrange the cooked pasta on a paper towel and allow to cool.

Place the cooked Pappardelle in a serving bowl a few at a time, while adding sauce. Continue to alternate between adding the pasta and sauce until you have used all the pasta. Top the pasta with additional sauce and garnish with the fresh grated cheese and serve.

BAKED TUNA FILLED SCRIPPELLE

TONNO SCRIPPELLE AL FORNO

"Throughout Italy, cannelloni is traditionally made with pasta dough. However, many Abruzzese cooks have substituted scrippelles for a more regional taste." – Elisa

SERVES 4–6 PEOPLE

INGREDIENTS

- 3 cups ricotta cheese, well-drained
- 2 cups fresh Pecorino Romano or Parmesan cheese, grated
- 10 ounces white albacore tuna
- ¼ cup pistachios, crushed
- ¼ cup black olives, chopped
- 1 tablespoon capers
- 1 cup Italian-style breadcrumbs
- 10–12 freshly prepared Scrippelle crêpes, see my recipe in Pastas, pg.64
- 1 cup unsalted butter, melted

DIRECTIONS

Preheat oven to 350 degrees F.

In a medium glass mixing bowl, add the ricotta, tuna, olives, capers, pistachios and grated cheese; reserving some grated cheese for garnish. Mix thoroughly with a wooden spoon. Lay a Scrippelle on a clean surface and fill with 2 tablespoons of the mixture along one side, lengthwise. Roll the Scrippelle starting with the filling side and tuck the ends under the bottom. Place them in a buttered 13 x 9 x 2-inch glass casserole dish. Pour the melted butter over the tops and garnish with the remaining cheese and breadcrumbs. Bake in the oven for 30 minutes. Remove from the oven, plate, and serve.

BAKED RIGATONI

PASTA AL FORNO

SERVES 6-8 PEOPLE

INGREDIENTS

- 1½ pound of rigatoni
- ½ pound mozzarella cheese, shredded
- 3 28-ounce cans crushed tomatoes
- 1 onion, sliced in half
- ½ cup fresh basil, chopped
- ½ cup fresh parsley, chopped, including the stem
- Salt and fresh black pepper to taste
- ½ cup Pecorino Romano cheese, grated

DIRECTIONS

In a medium stock pan, add the olive oil and garlic and simmer over medium heat for 2-3 minutes. Add the onion halves, 1 cup of water, and the tomatoes. Add the basil, parsley, and a pinch of salt and pepper. Simmer on low heat, uncovered for 1 hour until reduced.

Preheat oven to 350 degrees F.

Prepare a large stockpot of water with a pinch of salt and bring to a boil. Cook the pasta only half the recommended time on the box. Drain the pasta and place in a large glass bowl. Mix in 2-3 cups of the tomato sauce and the mozzarella and blend into the pasta. Coat the bottom of a glass casserole pan with a spoonful of sauce. Add the pasta mixture to the baking pan. Cover with the Pecorino cheese and a generous helping of the tomato sauce. Bake uncovered for 30 minutes until the top is golden brown. Remove from the oven and serve.

PAPPARDELLE WITH ARTICHOKES

PAPPARDELLE CON CARCIOFI

SERVES 4–6 PEOPLE

INGREDIENTS:

For the Sauce:

- 4 fresh artichokes
- 1 cup salted butter
- 1 cup dry white wine
- 1 cup chicken stock
- 2 garlic cloves, chopped
- ½ cup olive oil
- ¼ cup fresh parsley, chopped including the stem
- Salt & fresh black pepper to taste
- ½ cup Pecorino Romano cheese, grated

FOR THE PASTA:

- 1 portion fresh egg pasta strips, see my recipe in Pastas, pg.52

DIRECTIONS:

Bring a large stockpot of water with a pinch of salt to a boil.

Clean the artichokes by stripping off the outer leaves, removing the fuzz from the choke, and then slice them. Place the slices in a bowl of water.

In a medium-sized sauté pan, heat the oil and butter over medium heat until the butter has melted. Add the garlic and sauté for 3-5 minutes. Drain the artichokes and add to the sauté pan mixing the butter and artichokes thoroughly. Add the wine and chicken stock, cover, and simmer on low to medium heat for 30 minutes. Check that the pan is maintaining liquid; if not, add more chicken stock.

While the artichokes are cooking, prepare the pasta. From the hand-rolled or machine-pressed fresh egg pasta dough you prepared, cut 3-inch long by 1½-inch wide rectangular strips of dough with a knife or cutting wheel. The water should be boiling by now, so drop 3-4 strips of dough into the boiling water at a time, cook for 1–2 minutes and remove with a handheld strainer. Arrange the cooked pasta on a paper towel and allow to cool.

Place the cooked Pappardelle in a serving bowl a few at a time while adding some of the sauce. Continue to alternate between adding the pasta and sauce until you have used all the pasta. Top off the pasta with additional sauce and garnish with the fresh grated cheese and serve.

TAGLIATELLE WITH BLACK TRUFFLES

TAGLIATELLE CON TARTUFO

SERVES 4-6 PEOPLE

INGREDIENTS

FOR THE SAUCE:
- 1 cup unsalted butter
- ½ cup fresh Parmesan cheese, grated
- Fresh grated Black Truffles

FOR THE PASTA:
- 1 portion fresh egg pasta strips, see my recipe in Pastas, pg.52

DIRECTIONS

Prepare the Pasta:

Bring a large stockpot of water with a pinch of salt to a boil.

Roll out the fresh egg pasta into 10-inch long strips by 4-inch wide. Roll them tightly and using a sharp knife slice the roll into ½-inch wide slices.

Pasta water should be boiling by now, so drop the pasta into the boiling water and cook for 3-4 minutes. Remove with a handheld strainer and set aside in a bowl.

Prepare the Sauce:

Melt the butter in a large sauté pan and add the drained pasta along with a little pasta water. Add the Parmesan cheese and grated truffles, and cook everything together for 2-3 minutes, until the sauce thickens. Transfer the pasta to a serving bowl and garnish with more cheese and grated truffle.

LINGUINE WITH ONIONS

LINGUINE CON CIPOLLE

SERVES 6-8 PEOPLE

INGREDIENTS

- 1 portion fresh egg linguine, see my recipe in Pastas, pg.52 or 1lb of box pasta
- 2 Italian sweet sausages, optional, remove from casing and finely chopped
- 3 large yellow onions, finely chopped
- ¾ cup olive oil
- 3 tomatoes, finely diced
- 1½ cup whole milk
- Salt and fresh black pepper to taste
- Fresh Pecorino Romano cheese, grated for garnish

"In the last years of Francesco's life, he spent more and more time in the kitchen, surprising me with dinner on the table when I returned home from work. This was one of his favorite dishes to prepare." – Elisa

DIRECTIONS

Fill a large stockpot with water and a pinch of salt and bring to a boil. Place an extra large sauté pan over medium heat. Add the olive oil; then add the onion and sausage and sauté approximately 5 minutes until the onions are tender.

Reduce the heat and add the milk and tomatoes and sauté for 5 minutes. Drop in the fresh egg linguine you have prepared and cook for 3-5 minutes. (If you are using dry pasta, cook half the recommended time according to box instructions.)

Remove the pasta from the stockpot and add to the sauté pan. Increase the heat and add a pinch of salt and pepper mix the pasta and onion mixture thoroughly. Sauté for an additional 4-6 minutes, remove from heat and transfer to a serving bowl. Garnish with Pecorino Romano cheese and serve.

GNOCCHI WITH RICOTTA CHEESE

GNOCCHI DI RICOTTA

SERVES 6 PEOPLE

YOU WILL NEED TO PREPARE MY FRESH TOMATO SAUCE OR CREAM SAUCE FOR SERVING.

INGREDIENTS

- 3 pounds ricotta Cheese, drained
- 3 eggs
- ½ cup olive oil
- 1 teaspoon salt
- 1 cup fresh Pecorino Romano cheese, grated
- 3 pounds all-purpose flour

DIRECTIONS

On a clean wooden or marble-like surface, make a mound of flour. Make a hole in the middle of the flour mound and add the eggs and olive oil to the center. Beat the eggs with a fork and then add the ricotta, salt and cheese. Fold in the flour with your hands. Work the dough forming a ball but make sure it does not stick to the surface. Lightly flour the surface, and pull a handful of the dough off the ball and roll with your fingertips into a 1-foot long snake. Cut the dough diagonally into 1-inch pieces.

Bring a large stockpot of water with a pinch of salt to a boil. Drop the gnocchi into the boiling water and cook for 5 minutes. They will rise to the top. Remove with hand strainer and drain thoroughly. Place in a serving bowl and add the sauce you have prepared. Garnish with more grated cheese and serve.

"The Laga truffle (both black and white) is one of the most precious and sought-after products in cooking, typically Italian, but used in cuisines all over the world. I remember the men leaving very early in the morning to search for these treasures. Many of my nephews still enjoy this hobby today." – Elisa

MEAT TORTELLINI

TORTELLINI DI CARNE

SERVES 4-6 PEOPLE

INGREDIENTS

FOR THE DOUGH:

- 5 eggs
- 2 cups all-purpose flour
- ¼ cup olive oil

FOR THE FILLING:

- 3 ounces lean pork
- 2 ounces chicken breast
- 2 ounces ground veal
- ¼ cup unsalted butter
- ½ cup fresh Pecorino Romano or Parmesan cheese, grated
- 1 pinch nutmeg
- 1 egg
- Salt and fresh black pepper, I recommend a pinch of each

YOU WILL NEED TO PREPARE CHICKEN OR BEEF STOCK TO SERVE THE TORTELLINI AS A SOUP OR SERVE WITH MY FRESH CREAM BASED OR TOMATO SAUCES.

DIRECTIONS

Prepare the filling:

Melt the butter in a large sauté pan over low heat. Chop the meats into small pieces. You can also use ground meats, which can sometimes be easier. Sauté the meats in the melted butter for roughly 10-15 minutes. Place the meats in a food processor and chop. Add the egg, grated cheese, salt, pepper, and nutmeg and blend together. Set the mixture aside.

Prepare the dough:

On a clean wooden or marble-like surface, make a mound of flour, make a hole in the middle and add the eggs with a tablespoon of olive oil. Beat the eggs with a fork, and gradually add the flour to the eggs. It will start to form dough. Incorporate the remaining flour to the mixture with your hands. Knead the dough until it is smooth. Divide the dough into 4–5 pieces and cover the pieces you are not working with immediately.

Pass each piece of dough through the largest setting of your pasta machine twice. Gradually pass it through the smaller settings to make it thinner and thinner, until you reach the thinnest level and pass it trough twice. You may have to dust with flour whenever the dough starts to stick. Lay out your sheets of pasta, and cut into 1½-inch squares.

Filling your pasta:

Spoon ½ teaspoon of filling onto the center of the squares. Close the squares by joining 2 opposite angles together to create a triangle. Press the ends together to secure them shut. Leave the long edge of the triangle on top and join the sides. Fold angles together, bringing them together to form a ring shape. Press the sides together to complete the seal.

Set the tortellini on a dry cloth for 1 hour to dry.

Options for serving:

If you are preparing as a soup, drop the tortellini into the stock for 4 minutes and serve with some grated cheese. Sometimes I will add ½-inch cubes of carrots and celery to my broth for a lovely presentation.

If you are serving with a tomato or cream sauce, you will need to boil the tortellini in water for 3-5 minutes, drain and then add the sauce. Garnish with grated cheese.

**MEAT
TORTELLINI**

**TORTELLINI
DI CARNE**

PENNE WITH BROCCOLI RABE

PENNE CON BROCCOLI DI RAPE

SERVES 4–6 PEOPLE

INGREDIENTS

- 1 pound fresh broccoli rabe
- ⅓ cup Kalamata olives, pitted and sliced
- 4 garlic cloves, sliced
- ½ teaspoon crushed red pepper flakes
- 3 tablespoons olive oil
- 1 pound dry penne pasta
- ½ cup fresh Parmesan cheese, shredded

DIRECTIONS

Bring a large stockpot of water with a pinch of salt to a boil.

Rinse the broccoli rabe under cold water and chop into 1-inch pieces. Once the pot of water has come to a boil, blanch the broccoli rabe for 1-2 minutes. Remove the broccoli using a slotted spoon and drain. Save ¼ cup of the water. Drop the pasta into the boiling water and cook al dente according to the box instructions.

In a large skillet, heat the olive oil over medium heat. Add the garlic, olives and crushed red pepper, sauté until the garlic is tender for 2-3 minutes. Add the broccoli rabe and the ¼ cup of water saved from the boiling pot and continue to sauté for 3-5 minutes. Drain the penne and add to the skillet tossing with the broccoli rabe for 2 minutes. Remove from heat and transfer to a serving bowl. Garnish with Parmesan cheese and serve.

SPAGHETTI WITH EGGPLANT

SPAGHETTI CON LE MELANZANE

SERVES 4–6 PEOPLE

INGREDIENTS

- 6 eggplants
- 2 garlic cloves, crushed
- 2 teaspoons salt
- 2 pounds fresh tomatoes, or 2 cans crushed tomatoes
- 1 onion, sliced in half
- ½ cup fresh parsley, chopped, including the stem
- ½ cup basil, finely chopped
- Additional salt and fresh black pepper to taste
- 1 cup vegetable oil
- ¼ cup olive oil
- 1 cup fresh Pecorino Romano or Parmesan cheese, grated
- 1 portion fresh egg spaghetti, see my recipe in Pastas, pg.52 or 1lb box pasta

DIRECTIONS

Prepare the sauce by heating the olive oil and garlic in a medium saucepan over medium heat. Sauté the garlic for 2-3 minutes and add the onion. Peel and chop fresh tomatoes, remove seeds, and add to the saucepan. Add parsley, basil, salt, and pepper to taste. Allow to cook for at least 30 minutes. Remove the onion before serving.

Peel and slice the eggplants into very thin slices. Place in a colander and sprinkle with the salt. Toss and allow to sit for 1 hour to drain the juices.

Heat vegetable oil in a medium sauté pan over medium heat. Before adding the eggplant a few at a time to the skillet, wipe them dry. Fry them on both sides until brown on both sides, and drain on a paper towel-lined wire rack.

Bring a large stockpot of water with a pinch of salt to a boil. Drop the pasta into the boiling water and cook accordingly: 3-4 minutes for fresh pasta, 10-12 minutes for boxed pasta. Drain pasta and place in a large serving bowl. Add cooked eggplant, half the cheese, and sauce to the pasta and toss. Garnish with the remaining cheese and some fresh parsley to serve.

ANGEL HAIR WITH ANCHOVIES

CAPELLI D'ANGELI CON ACCIUGHE

SERVES 4–6 PEOPLE

INGREDIENTS:

- 1 large eggplant, peeled and cubed
- 6 large fresh tomatoes, peeled and chopped
- 2 sweet peppers
- 3-4 anchovy fillets
- ½ cup black olives, pitted and halved
- 4 teaspoons capers
- ½ cup olive oil
- ½ cup fresh basil, finely chopped
- Salt and fresh black pepper
- 1 pound box angel hair pasta

DIRECTIONS:

Preheat oven to 350 degrees F.

Slice the peppers in half and remove the seeds. Place them on a baking sheet and bake in the oven for 15-20 minutes until the skin begins to blister. Remove from the oven and peel the skin and cut into very fine strips.

Peel and cut the eggplant into 1-inch by 1-inch cubes. Place in a colander and add some salt. Toss and allow to sit for 1 hour to drain off the juices.

In a large sauté pan, heat the olive oil over medium heat and sauté garlic for 2-3 minutes. Add tomatoes and eggplant with a pinch of salt and sauté for 20 minutes. Add the pepper slices and some black pepper and continue to simmer. Wash the anchovy fillets and remove the bones. Chop the anchovy fillets into small pieces and add them to the pan with the olives, capers, and basil. Cover the pan and continue to cook for an additional 10-15 minutes. Add some water if the tomatoes show signs of sticking to the pan.

Bring a large stockpot of water with a pinch of salt to a boil. Drop pasta into the boiling water and cook according to the box instructions. Drain pasta and place in a large serving bowl. Add sauce to the pasta and toss.

SPAGHETTI WITH CRABS

SPAGHETTI CON GRANCHI

SERVES 4-6 PEOPLE

INGREDIENTS:

- 3 pounds fresh crabs
- 1 cup olive oil
- ½ cup fresh parsley, chopped including the stem
- 3-4 garlic cloves, chopped
- ½ cup dry white wine
- 4 pounds fresh tomatoes peeled and chopped, or 3 28-ounce cans of crushed tomatoes.
- Salt and fresh black pepper to taste
- 1 portion fresh egg spaghetti, see my recipe in Pastas, pg.52 or 1lb box pasta

DIRECTIONS:

Heat the olive oil in heavy large saucepan over medium heat. Add garlic and sauté until tender, about 3 minutes. Add the parsley, wine, and crabs and sauté for 30 minutes. Add fresh or canned tomatoes. If you are using canned tomatoes, add 1 cup of water. Simmer for 1½ hours on low heat. Add additional water if needed.

Bring a large stockpot of water with a pinch of salt to a boil. Drop pasta into the boiling water and cook accordingly: 3-5 minutes for fresh pasta, or follow box instructions for dry pasta. Drain pasta and place in a large serving bowl.

Add the sauce and toss with the pasta. Garnish with the crabs from the sauce and serve.

SPAGHETTI WITH TUNA MARINARA SAUCE

SPAGHETTI CON TONNO ALLA MARINARA

SERVES 4-6 PEOPLE

INGREDIENTS:

- 1 5-ounce can light tuna in water, drained well
- 2 medium onions, chopped
- 1 28-ounce can crushed tomatoes
- A pinch of salt
- ½ cup fresh basil, roughly chopped
- Fresh black pepper to taste
- 1 portion fresh egg spaghetti, see my recipe in Pastas, pg.52 or 1lb box pasta

DIRECTIONS:

Heat the olive oil in large sauté pan over medium heat. Add garlic and sauté until tender, about 5 minutes. Add the basil, tuna, and crushed tomatoes and sauté for 30–40 minutes. Add some water if necessary.

Bring a large stockpot of water with a pinch of salt to a boil. Drop pasta into the boiling water and cook accordingly: 3-5 minutes for fresh pasta, or follow box instructions for dry pasta. Drain pasta and place in a large serving bowl. Add sauce and toss.

SPAGHETTI WITH ARTICHOKE HEARTS

SPAGHETTI CON CUORI DI CARCIOFI

SERVES 4-6 PEOPLE

INGREDIENTS

- ½ cup olive oil
- 3 garlic cloves, chopped
- 1 large onion, chopped
- 2 fresh bay leaves, chopped
- ¼ cup fresh parsley, chopped, including the stem
- 1 14¾-ounce jar marinated artichoke hearts or frozen artichokes
- 1 portion fresh egg spaghetti, see my recipe in Pastas, pg.52 or 1lb box pasta
- ½ cup fresh Parmesan cheese, grated
- Salt and fresh black pepper to taste

DIRECTIONS

Bring a large stockpot of water with a pinch of salt to a boil. Heat the olive oil in a large, heavy saucepan over medium heat. Add onion and garlic and sauté until tender, about 5 minutes.

Add the artichokes, bay leaves and parsley and sauté for 2 minutes. Drop pasta into the boiling water and cook accordingly: 3-5 minutes for fresh pasta, or follow box instructions for dry pasta. Drain pasta and place in a large serving bowl. Add the artichoke mixture and toss. Garnish with salt and pepper and Parmesan cheese.

**SPAGHETTI WITH
ARTICHOKE HEARTS**

**SPAGHETTI CON
CUORI DI CARCIOFI**

RICOTTA RAVIOLI
RAVIOLI DI RICOTTA

INGREDIENTS:

- Prepare my Fresh Egg Pasta Dough, see my recipe in Pastas, pg.52
- 3 pounds Ricotta Cheese, drained
- 3 eggs
- ½ cup cooked and chopped fresh spinach, optional
- ½ cup fresh Pecorino Romano or Parmesan cheese, grated

DIRECTIONS:

Bring a large stockpot of water with a pinch of salt to a boil.

In a glass bowl, beat the egg, add the Ricotta cheese and grated cheese, and mix thoroughly. If you choose to include spinach, add with the grated cheese. Spread the strips of pasta dough on a clean surface dusted with flour. Starting 3 inches from one end, drop a tablespoon of the mixture in the center of the dough, and continue to drop every 3 inches. Fold over the pasta dough and press down on the ends where the pasta dough meets with your fingers. Using a wheel cutter, cut the Ravioli into moon shapes with the tablespoon of ricotta centered on each cut. Drop 4-6 Ravioli at a time into the boiling water for 5-7 minutes, and scoop out with a ladle and transfer to serving dish or plates.

"When it comes to selecting a pasta dish for the holidays, although the men prefer a generous bowl of spaghetti, my granddaughters Amanda and Lily prefer my Ravioli. So what does a grandmother do? She prepares both, so that everyone gathered at the table is happy." - Elisa

SPAGHETTI WITH MEATBALLS

SPAGHETTI CON POLPETTE

SERVES 6-8 PEOPLE

YOU WILL NEED TO PREPARE MY MINI MEATBALL OR CLASSIC MEATBALLS, AS WELL AS MY TOMATO MARINARA SAUCE PRIOR TO COOKING THIS DISH.

INGREDIENTS

- 1 portion mini or classic meatballs, see my recipes in Meats, pg.146
- 1 portion tomato marinara sauce, see my recipe in Sauces, pg.126
- 1 portion fresh egg pasta, see my recipe in Pastas, pg.52 or 1 pound box pasta
- Fresh Pecorino Romano or Parmesan cheese, grated

DIRECTIONS

Heat tomato sauce until it comes to a boil. Then reduce the heat, and add the mini or classic meatballs and ¼ cup of water. Continue to simmer for 1½ hours until the sauce thickens.

Bring a large stockpot of water with a pinch of salt to a boil. Drop pasta into the boiling water and cook accordingly: 3-5 minutes for fresh pasta, or follow box instructions for dry pasta. Drain pasta and place in a large serving bowl.

Use a slotted spoon to remove mini meatballs. Spread them evenly over the pasta. Then ladle some sauce over the pasta and garnish with cheese. Once you have brought this to the table, serve to each guest and toss each plate individually. Have some extra sauce with meatballs to serve. If you choose to serve classic meatballs, you should remove all the meatballs from the sauce and serve them separately in their own serving bowl. Toss pasta, sauce, and cheese before serving to your guests. Pass the meatballs around the table and allow each guest to help themselves.

"Traditionally we would prepare this dish with mini meatballs rather than the more contemporary meatballs which have become so famous around the world." - Elisa

CLASSIC MANICOTTI

SERVES 4-6 PEOPLE

INGREDIENTS

- 32 ounces whole milk ricotta cheese, drained well
- ½ cup fresh Pecorino Romano cheese, grated
- 3 eggs
- ¼ cup fresh parsley, chopped, including the stem
- 1 cup fresh mozzarella, shredded
- A pinch of salt and fresh black pepper
- 1 portion fresh egg pasta sheets, see my recipe in Pastas, pg.52
- Fresh tomato marinara sauce, see my recipe in Sauces, pg.126

DIRECTIONS

Prepare a pot of my fresh tomato marinara sauce and a portion of my fresh egg pasta. Cut the pasta sheets into 6-inch long pieces. Bring a large stockpot of water with a pinch of salt to a boil. Drop pasta into the boiling water and remove as soon as they rise to the surface. Dip the cooked sheets in a bowl of cold water, then lay on a kitchen towel to dry.

Preheat oven to 350 degrees F.

In a glass mixing bowl add the ricotta, ¼ cup Pecorino cheese, parsley, mozzarella cheese, salt and pepper, and mix well. In a separate bowl, beat the eggs, add them to the cheese mixture and mix thoroughly.

Line the cut pasta sheets on a clean surface and add 2 tablespoons of the mixture along the long end of the pasta sheet. Roll the end with the mixture like a log. Add a layer of the marinara sauce to a 13 x 9 x 2-inch glass casserole dish, and lay the wrapped manicotti together tightly in the dish with the seam side down.

Once all the manicotti has been lined up in the dish, cover generously with more marinara sauce, and sprinkle the remaining ¼ cup of grated Pecorino cheese over the sauce. Cover the pan with aluminum foil and poke a few holes in the foil. Bake the manicotti for 30 minutes. Remove from the oven and allow the manicotti to cool for 5-10 minutes to avoid breaking them when removing to serve. Garnish with more grated cheese and fresh parsley.

CLASSIC LASAGNA

SERVES 8-10 PEOPLE

INGREDIENTS

- 1 pound ground lean beef
- 1 small onion, chopped
- 1 garlic clove, chopped
- ¼ cup olive oil
- 2 pounds fresh mozzarella cheese, shredded
- 1 cup fresh Parmesan cheese, grated
- 2 eggs
- Pinch of salt and fresh black pepper
- ¼ cup fresh parsley, finely chopped including the stem
- ¼ cup milk
- 3 portions fresh egg pasta sheets, see my recipe in Pastas, pg.52
- Fresh tomato marinara sauce, see my recipe in Sauces, pg.126

DIRECTIONS

Prepare a pot of my fresh tomato marinara sauce and 3 portions of my fresh egg pasta. Bring a large stockpot of water with a pinch of salt to a boil. Drop pasta into the boiling water and remove as soon as it rises to the surface. Dip the cooked sheets in a bowl of cold water, then lay on a kitchen towel to dry.

Preheat oven to 350 degrees F.

In a medium sauté pan, heat the olive oil over medium heat and sauté the onion and garlic until the onions are soft. Add the ground meat, salt, pepper, and parsley, and continue to sauté until the meat is brown. Drain the oil and set the meat aside. In a separate bowl, beat the eggs and milk.

Assembling the Lasagna:

Add a layer of sauce to the base of a 13 x 9 x 2-inch glass casserole pan. Line the pan with layers of pasta sheets, overlapping them slightly. Brush the sheets with the egg mixture. Add a layer of sauce, sprinkle with ground meat, and top with mozzarella and Parmesan cheese. Repeat this process until you have reached the top layer which should be brushed with some sauce and grated cheese.

Bake for 60-90 minutes covered. Remove from the oven and allow to sit for 20 minutes before serving.

SALADS AND VEGETABLES

**BROCCOLI
RABE**

RAPINI

SEE PAGE 100

SAUTÉED MIXED VEGETABLES

VEGETALI MISTI SALTATI

SERVES 4-6 PEOPLE

INGREDIENTS:

- 1 eggplant, peeled and cubed
- 3 green zucchini, sliced
- 1 green pepper, seeded and sliced into strips about ½ inch thick
- ½ head of fennel, sliced into strips about ½ inch thick
- 3-4 fresh tomatoes, cubed
- 1 large white onion, sliced
- 2 cloves garlic, chopped
- ¼ cup olive oil
- 1 teaspoon fresh basil, chopped
- 2 teaspoons fresh parsley, chopped
- 1 teaspoon salt
- 1 teaspoon crushed red pepper
- 1 teaspoon fresh black pepper

DIRECTIONS:

In a large sauté pan, combine olive oil, onions, and garlic and heat until onions have a nice, light brown color. Add all the ingredients except the herbs. Mix gently and cook for 5 minutes. Add the herbs, a cup of water and cover with lid. Cook on low heat for 45 minutes, stirring every 5-10 minutes. Remove cover and allow to cook uncovered until liquid evaporates, and cook to desired thickness and consistency.

STRING BEAN SALAD

INSALATA DI FAGIOLINI

SERVES 4-6 PEOPLE

INGREDIENTS:

- 2 pounds fresh string beans
- 2 garlic cloves, chopped
- ¼ cup olive oil
- 1 tablespoon red wine vinegar
- 2 teaspoons salt

DIRECTIONS:

Wash and clip off the ends of the string beans. Fill a medium saucepan ¾ of the way with water. Once water begins to boil drop the string beans into the water and cook for 10-15 minutes, depending on whether you prefer your beans soft or al dente.

Drain the string beans well and allow them to cool for 10 minutes. In a mixing bowl, add the beans, chopped garlic, 1 teaspoon of salt, olive oil and vinegar and toss like a salad and serve.

FENNEL
FINOCCHIO

INGREDIENTS:

- 4 bulbs of fennel
- ½ cup olive oil
- 1 teaspoon black pepper

DIRECTIONS:

Wash the bulbs of fennel well, quarter them, and rinse them again, checking to make sure that no dirt has worked its way in between the sections. Slice them finely, or julienne them. Arrange the slices of fennel on a small serving plate. Place oil and pepper in a small bowl for dipping.

STRING BEANS WITH TOMATOES

FAGIOLINI CON POMODORO

SERVES 4-6 PEOPLE

INGREDIENTS:

- 2 pounds fresh string beans
- 2-3 garlic cloves, chopped
- ½ cup olive oil
- 4 cups fresh tomatoes, sliced or 28 ounce can of whole tomatoes.
- Salt to taste

DIRECTIONS:

Wash and clip off the ends of the string beans. Fill a medium saucepan with water. Once water begins to boil drop the string beans into the water and cook for 10-15 minutes.

Remove string beans and drain well. In a sauté pan, heat olive oil and garlic and fry for 2-3 minutes. Then add the slices of tomatoes or can of whole tomatoes and drop the string beans on top of the tomatoes and cook together for 15 minutes, stirring occasionally. Add salt to taste and serve.

STRING BEANS WITH POTATOES

FAGIOLINI CON PATATE

SERVES 4-6 PEOPLE

DIRECTIONS:

Wash and clip off the ends of the string beans. Peel and cut the potatoes into 4-6 pieces. In a large saucepan bring 16-20 cups of water to boil. Drop the string beans and potatoes into the water and add a teaspoon of salt. Boil for 30 minutes until beans and potatoes are soft.

Drain the water from the saucepan and set the string beans and potatoes aside in a bowl. Return the saucepan to burner and add the olive oil and garlic. Fry the garlic until golden brown and remove from heat. Pour the string beans and potatoes into the saucepan and add a teaspoon of salt. Using a wooden spoon or spatula, chop the string beans and potatoes in an up and down motion, mashing them together. Place in serving bowl and serve.

INGREDIENTS:

- 2 pounds fresh string beans
- 5 Idaho potatoes, peel and cut each into 4-6 pieces
- 1 cup olive oil
- 3 garlic cloves, chopped
- 2 teaspoons of salt

"After I married Francesco and moved to his hometown of San Massimo, I spent the first few months in the kitchen with my new mother-in-law learning their traditions in the kitchen and this was one of the first dishes she shared with me." – Elisa

FRIED PEAS
PISELLI FRITTI

SERVES 4-6 PEOPLE

"Fried peas served alongside my chicken or lamb cutlets is a favorite of my daughter-in-law, Tina. Irish by blood, but Italian by palate." – Elisa

INGREDIENTS:

- 1 16-ounce bag frozen peas
- 1 large white onion, sliced or chopped
- ½ cup water
- ¼ cup olive oil
- 1 teaspoon salt
- 1 pinch of fresh ground black pepper

DIRECTIONS:

In a medium frying pan, add water, oil and onions, and let simmer for 3-5 minutes. Then add the peas, salt, and pepper, mixing occasionally until liquid evaporates. Sauté for an additional 5 minutes stirring constantly and remove from heat.

RICE WITH ONIONS & MUSHROOMS
RISO CON CIPOLLE E FUNGHI

SERVES 4-6 PEOPLE

INGREDIENTS:

- ½ cup olive oil
- 1 pound mushrooms, finely chopped
- ¼ cup butter
- 1 pound Carolina rice
- 2 large white onions, finely chopped
- 1 cup chicken stock

DIRECTIONS:

Cook rice following the directions on the package. In a small saucepan, boil the mushrooms for 5 minutes. In a large sauté pan over medium heat, sauté olive oil and onions until the onions are golden. Drain and add mushrooms to the sauté pan. Drain rice and add it to the sauté pan. Add the butter and chicken stock and sauté for an additional 5-8 minutes. Remove from heat and serve.

BROCCOLI RABE

RAPINI

SERVES 4-6 PEOPLE

INGREDIENTS:

- 2 pounds fresh broccoli rabe, trim the ends
- 3 garlic cloves, sliced into quarters
- ¼ cup olive oil
- Salt and fresh black pepper to taste

DIRECTIONS:

Bring a large pot of salted water to boil. Add the broccoli rabe and boil for 10 minutes. Cook until tender but still firm. In a large sauté pan, add the olive oil and garlic and sauté the garlic until lightly brown. Drain the broccoli rabe and add to the sauté pan and sauté for 5 minutes.

POTATO LASAGNA

TIMBALLO DI PATATE

SERVES 8-10 PEOPLE

INGREDIENTS:

- 5 pounds Idaho potatoes
- 24-30 Scrippelle crêpes, see my recipe in pastas, pg.64
- 4 cups mozzarella cheese, shredded
- 2 eggs
- 1 cup Pecorino Romano, grated
- 1 cup Parmesan cheese, grated
- ½ pound pancetta, diced
- ¼ cup fresh parsley, finely chopped
- 2 teaspoons salt
- 1 teaspoon fresh black pepper

DIRECTIONS:

Preheat oven to 400 degrees F.

Prepare a batch of Scrippelle from my recipe. Fill a large saucepan with water and boil the potatoes whole until they are tender. Remove the potatoes from the water, but do not discard the water from the pot. Peel the potatoes and set aside in a large glass mixing bowl. In a small mixing bowl, beat the eggs. Mash the potatoes with a masher or fork, as I do, and pour in the beaten eggs, mozzarella, grated cheeses, and prosciutto and mix well. Blend in the parsley, salt, and pepper.

Grease a 13 x 9 x 2-inch glass casserole dish with olive oil or butter.

Add a thin layer of the pot water in the casserole dish and place a layer of the Scrippelle. Using a spatula, layer the potato mixture evenly across the Scrippelles. Add another layer of Scrippelles, some water from the pot, and the mixture. Continue this process until you have reached the top layer. Wet the top layer with the water from the pot, add some grated cheese and bake for 20-25 minutes. The top should be golden brown and crisp.

GRILLED EGGPLANT

MELANZANE ARROSTO

SERVES 4-6 PEOPLE

INGREDIENTS:

- 2 pounds eggplants, peeled, sliced
- 2 garlic cloves, chopped
- ½ cup olive oil
- Salt to taste

DIRECTIONS:

Preheat oven to 350 degrees F.

Peel and slice the eggplants from top to bottom into ½-inch slices. Grease a roasting pan with olive oil and layer the slices of eggplant in the pan. Place in the oven and cook for 20-25 minutes to desired tenderness. Remove the eggplant and cool to room temperature. Slice each piece of eggplant again, now ¼-inch pieces, and place in a large serving bowl. Add the garlic, olive oil, and salt, mix thoroughly and serve.

VEGETABLE MEDLEY

SERVES 6-8 PEOPLE

INGREDIENTS:

- 1 pound broccoli florets
- 2 large onions, sliced
- 1 pound cauliflower florets
- 3 garlic cloves, chopped
- 1 pound green beans
- 1 cup olive oil
- 1 pound green peas
- 2 cups water
- 1 pound carrots, peeled and sliced
- Salt and fresh black pepper to taste

DIRECTIONS:

In a large sauté pan, add all the ingredients and sauté over medium heat until the water evaporates, roughly 30 minutes. Reduce the heat to low, add a pinch of salt and pepper, cover, and continue to cook the vegetables until they have reached desired tenderness. Remove from heat and serve.

ROASTED POTATOES

PATATE AL FORNO

SERVES 4-6 PEOPLE

INGREDIENTS:

- 6 large Idaho potatoes, peeled and thickly sliced
- 1 tablespoon salt
- 1 cup olive oil
- 1 tablespoon fresh rosemary
- 1 teaspoon fresh black pepper

DIRECTIONS:

Preheat oven to 350 degrees F.

Peel and slice the potatoes. Each potato should yield 6 slices. Add the potatoes to a roasting pan. Pour the olive oil over the potatoes then sprinkle with rosemary, salt, and pepper and mix together with your hands. Place in the preheated oven and cook for 1 hour. Poke the potatoes with a fork to check if cooked thoroughly. Remove from oven and serve.

ROASTED POTATOES

PATATE AL FORNO

EGGPLANT PARMIGIANO

MELANZANE ALLA PARMIGIANA

SERVES 6-8 PEOPLE

INGREDIENTS

- 2 large eggplants
- 2 cups Italian-style breadcrumbs
- 3 eggs
- 2½ cups vegetable oil
- 2 cups peas
- 1 medium onion, chopped
- 2 cups mushrooms, chopped
- 2 cups fresh mozzarella cheese, shredded
- Salt and fresh black pepper to taste
- 1 portion of my fresh tomato sauce, see my recipe in Sauces, pg.126
- Fresh Parmesan cheese, grated

DIRECTIONS

In a medium sauté pan, heat ¼ of the oil over medium heat. Sauté the peas, onions, and mushrooms for approximately 15 minutes. Peel and slice the eggplant into ½-inch thick slices. Rinse the slices under cold water and pat dry with paper towels. Beat the eggs in a bowl, and pour the breadcrumbs into a separate bowl. Using the sauté pan, heat the remaining oil over medium heat. Dip the slices of eggplant into the beaten eggs, then the breadcrumbs, flipping them to coat evenly. Place in hot oil and fry for 2-3 minutes on each side. Remove the eggplant slices from the oil and place on a paper towel-covered wire rack.

Preheat oven to 350 degrees F.

Using a 13 x 9 x 2-inch glass casserole dish, ladle a thin layer of sauce on the bottom of the dish. Place a layer of the eggplant slices together tightly and sprinkle with Parmesan cheese. Add a layer of the peas and mushroom mixture, then a layer of cheese. Add more sauce and repeat the process, of layering eggplant, peas and mushrooms, cheese and sauce. You should have 3 complete layers. Sprinkle with salt and pepper and bake in the oven for 30 minutes.

Remove from the oven and serve from the casserole dish, or use a biscuit cutter to make circular pieces for a more formal presentation. Sprinkle with Parmesan cheese.

"This dish is the favorite of my granddaughter-in-law, Susanne. She is the first vegetarian in our family, so I always prepare this dish for her when she visits." - Elisa

EGGPLANT PARMIGIANO
MELANZANE ALLA PARMIGIANA

TOMATO, CUCUMBER & ONION SALAD

INSALATA DI POMODORO, CETRIOLO, E CIPOLLE

"This is my son-in-law Bob's favorite salad, after a few bowls of pasta." – Elisa

INGREDIENTS:

- 6 ripe tomatoes, cut into 6 even slices
- 1 large white onion, sliced
- 2 cucumbers, peeled and sliced into ½-inch slices
- ¼ cup olive oil
- 2 tablespoons red wine vinegar
- Salt to taste

DIRECTIONS:

Once you have sliced the tomatoes, cucumber and onions, place in a large serving bowl. Add the oil, vinegar, and a pinch or two of salt and toss.

EGGS IN PURGATORY

UOVA IN PURGATORIO

INGREDIENTS:

- 6 eggs
- ¼ cup olive oil
- 1 onion, chopped
- 2 garlic cloves, chopped
- 1 28-ounce can crushed tomatoes
- ¼ cup fresh parsley, chopped, including the stem
- Fresh Pecorino Romano or Parmesan cheese, grated
- Salt to taste
- ¼ cup fresh basil, chopped

DIRECTIONS:

In a large sauté pan, heat the olive oil over medium heat and add the garlic. Sauté the garlic for 2-3 minutes, and then add the onions. Sauté for an additional 5 minutes. Reduce the heat and pour in the tomatoes, parsley, basil, and ½ cup of water. Bring the tomatoes to a boil. Carefully crack the eggs into the pan, keeping them whole and separated. Add a pinch of salt, and increase the heat. Cook 5-7 minutes; you will see the whites of the eggs begin to set. It is difficult to remove this dish from the pan, so bring to the table and serve directly from the pan. Garnish with some cheese.

ITALIAN STUFFING

INGREDIENTS:

- 1 set gizzards and liver from a chicken or turkey
- 2 onions, chopped
- 3 celery stalks, chopped
- ½ cup fresh parsley, chopped, including the stem
- 2 carrots, peeled and chopped
- 3 garlic cloves, chopped
- ½ cup Italian-style breadcrumbs
- 6 cups Italian bread, cubed
- ½ cup chicken or turkey stock

DIRECTIONS:

In a medium saucepan, boil the gizzards and liver for 30 minutes. Drain them and chop them into small pieces and add them to a large glass bowl. Add in the bread cubes and stock and mix together. Add the onions, carrots, celery, garlic, parsley, and breadcrumbs and mix thoroughly with your hands. Refrigerate until you are ready to stuff the bird and roast it.

" This is the traditional way I and many of my friends would prepare stuffing when cooking a turkey. However, as the children got older and realized what some of the ingredients were, I had to make some adjustments by replacing the gizzards and liver with sausage and bacon. Or you can do what my friend Gina does, and use a food processor to grind the gizzards and liver and add them to the stuffing mixture with some bacon so the children don't notice." - Elisa

ITALIAN CABBAGE
CAPPUCCIO ITALIANO

SERVES 4-6 PEOPLE

INGREDIENTS:

- 4 pounds fresh Italian cabbage, shredded
- ¼ cup olive oil
- 3 garlic cloves, sliced into quarters
- Salt and fresh black pepper to taste

DIRECTIONS:

Bring a large pot of salted water to boil. Add the cabbage and boil for 20-25 minutes, cooking until tender. In a large sauté pan add the olive oil and garlic and sauté the garlic until lightly browned. Drain and add the cabbage to the pan with a pinch of salt and pepper. Sauté for 15-20 minutes.

BAKED EGGPLANT, PROSCIUTTO, AND TOMATOES

MELANZANE, PROSCIUTTO E POMODORI AL FORNO

SERVES 4-6 PEOPLE

INGREDIENTS

- 3 pounds eggplants, peeled and sliced
- ½ pound prosciutto, sliced thin
- ½ pound dry mozzarella, sliced
- 1 28-ounce can crushed tomatoes
- 2 garlic gloves, chopped
- 1 small onion, chopped
- ¼ cup fresh parsley, chopped, including the stem
- ½ cup olive oil
- ½ cup fresh Pecorino Romano or Parmesan cheese, grated
- Salt and fresh black pepper to taste
- ¼ cup fresh basil, whole

DIRECTIONS

In a medium saucepan, sauté the garlic with the olive oil over medium heat until golden. Add the tomatoes, parsley, basil, and a pinch of salt and pepper. Simmer the sauce for 30 minutes. While the sauce is cooking, prepare the eggplant.

Preheat oven to 350 degrees F.

Peel and slice the eggplants from top to bottom into ½-inch slices. Grease a roasting pan with olive oil and layer the slices of eggplant in the pan. Place in the oven and bake for 10 minutes to soften. Remove the eggplant and cool to room temperature.

Add one slice of cheese, then one slice of prosciutto, to the top of each piece of eggplant. Roll the eggplant and line them tightly in a roasting pan layered with some sauce. Add the remaining sauce to the top and garnish with grated cheese. Bake in the oven for 20-25 minutes.

FINDING SALVATION

Many people have asked me how I became a caretaker for children with special needs and how I came to this calling so late in my life. This story has a happy ending; however, this story is also a tale of the obstacles life puts in our way and how we can sometimes find joy as a result of tragedy.

I have confessed that I never wanted to leave Italy and never really thought of living in America. Once I arrived on these shores, I was certain that I would soon return home. Francesco and I, along with our young daughter, struggled to adapt to this foreign land. True, we had the comfort of living in a community of families in a similar situation, and we developed many friendships, some of which I still have to this day. But there is one hardship in particular that ensured I would never return to Italy.

My second daughter, Agnes, was tragically born with spina bifida. Here in America, we found good medical care for our fragile daughter. I have no doubt there were good doctors back in Italy who could have provided for our needs; but our hometowns did not have the kind of hospitals and services we found in America. And so, I quickly realized that I had been dealt a rather ironic fate: I was isolated and stuck in this foreign land, but at the same time, America was where I had access to the kind of resources I needed to care for my family.

So we stayed, determined to make a life for ourselves. Life was certainly not easy. Francesco worked very hard, and I helped out however I could. I served as his dutiful assistant, sometimes helping with the books or answering calls from customers in his contracting business. But I was also a helping hand, getting my hands dirty with the same construction work my husband performed so that we could have the essentials of life: a home, food, and clothing for our family.

I was also responsible for taking care of the household and raising our children. Having arrived in America with one child, then having our second daughter, it would be some years later that, a son, Frank, would arrive in our lives. I was somewhat depressed at the time, and many believe the birth of my son saved me from falling into clinical depression. So for many years, we lived humbly, struggling like most families to make our way in the world. Yet, all the while, we had the added responsibility of caring for our fragile daughter, Agnes.

Around the time of young Frank's first communion, Agnes grew very ill, and she had to be hospitalized. To say that I was worried sick would be an understatement. It was a confusing time; as I prepared for one joyous occasion involving one of my children, I also worried over the health of one of my other children.

At one point, I remember, we planned a party to celebrate Frank's communion, and I set out to make the mini meatballs I have talked about many times in this book—the recipe I learned back in Italy that we prepared for special occasions; the recipe I was following that fateful day I slipped out of my mourning clothes in order to honor the passing of my sister—to attend a dance where I would meet my first boyfriend; the same recipe I had prepared dozens if not hundreds of times in my life. This would be the last time I would ever make these mini meatballs until we started writing this book.

As we set about making plans for Frank's party, we learned the tragic news that our daughter was in failing health. Sadly, in May, 1981, just days after Frank's communion, we lost Agnes. She passed away quietly, but her memory has left an indelible impression on my heart, and the pain of her loss is still as vivid today as it was then.

I was heartbroken. Devastated. Life seemed impossible and unfair. For the first time in my life, I turned away from my faith, unsure why I was beset with this tragedy. I retreated from the comfort of my family. I did my best to continue caring for my husband and two other children, but I was lost without my second-born child. She was so sweet and innocent, and I still cannot imagine a reason that she had to be taken from us.

In the wake of this loss, our community of friends and family surrounded us, and they refused to let me slip too far inside my own loss for the second time in my life. One very special thing they did was to raise a collection to help support my children, Nadia and Frank. It was such a kind gesture, and so I decided to accept the money and offer it to my children—and this is when they gave me perhaps the best gift ever. Nadia, in college refused to take the money. Instead, Nadia insisted I donate the money to a cause in Agnes' memory.

Sometime in October of that year, I finally decided to make a donation in my daughter's name and memory to the Don Guanella Village for developmentally disabled children. After much delaying and stalling, one day I finally mustered the strength I would need to go to the school and make the donation. I got in my car early in the morning, not knowing that my life was about to change forever.

As I pulled up to the gates of Don Guanella, it felt as though the gates of heaven had opened before me. My spirit lifted for the first time in months. I felt a sense of belonging and purpose.

After all, who was I to fret and worry over my own life in the presence of these amazing children struggling to fit into a world they barely understood? I decided right then and there that I had to return to Don Guanella to put all that I had learned in life and do what little I could to help these struggling children and their families.

I met with Father Peter, the priest who presided over the school and handed him my donation. I also asked the priest for a job. I did not immediately tell my family about my experience, nor did I tell them that I had taken work—the first real job I ever really had in life. A few days later, I returned to Don Guanella, and today, 35 years after, I still go to work every day with the same sense of purpose that I felt so many years ago.

I continue to feel peace and tranquility and my heart still lifts every time I arrive at work, now at Divine Providence, the sister school of Don Guanella. I would like to think that I have done at least a little good over the years in this work and that I have helped the children cope with the world around them; but I am positive that I have received far more in return than I would ever be able to give in a hundred lifetimes. The smiles of these children saved me when I lost my daughter, and again after I lost my husband.

SOUPS

CHICKPEA SOUP
ZUPPA DI CECI

SEE PAGE 121

FRESH BROTHS

CHICKEN BROTH
BRODO DI POLLO

ALWAYS HAVE FRESH PECORINO ROMANO OR PARMESAN CHEESE ON HAND TO GARNISH YOUR SOUPS AND STEWS.

INGREDIENTS:

- 1 5-6 pound whole chicken, or chicken pieces on the bone
- 6 quarts water
- 1 large onion, peeled whole
- 2 celery stalks, snapped into thirds, including leaves
- 2 carrots, peeled and snapped in half
- Salt to taste

DIRECTIONS:

Rinse the chicken under cold water both inside and out and place in a large stockpot. Add 6 quarts of water and a pinch of salt. ¾ of the chicken should be covered with water. Bring the broth to a boil. Skim off the scum that rises to the surface. After the first hour, add the onion, celery, and carrots. Simmer for an additional 3 hours. Continue to skim off any scum that rises to the top. Drain the broth through a sieve into a soup tureen. I often remove and cool the chicken, then use it to prepare some chicken salad.

BEEF STOCK
BRODO DI MANZO

INGREDIENTS:

- 1 2-3 pound beef on the bone
- 4 quarts of water
- 1 large onion, peeled whole
- 1 large tomato, peeled and chopped
- 2 celery stalks, snapped into thirds, including leaves
- 2 carrots, peeled and snapped in half
- Salt and fresh black pepper to taste

DIRECTIONS:

Place the beef in a large stockpot. Add 6 quarts of water and a pinch of salt and pepper. ¾ of the beef should be covered with water. Bring the broth to a boil. After the first hour add the onion, celery, and carrots. Simmer for an additional 3 hours. Drain the stock through a sieve into your soup tureen or jar for making gravies later.

VEGETABLE STOCK
ZUPPA VEGETALE

" I never used vegetable stock for soups until I married my husband and moved into his parents' home in San Massimo. Their town was not as rural as mine and farmers concentrated more on farming vegetables and olive oil than raising livestock. I learned many new recipes from my mother-in-law, and she watched over me to make sure I learned how to prepare her only son's favorites just right!" - Elisa

INGREDIENTS:

- 4 quarts water
- 2 potatoes, peeled and cut into halves
- 3 large onions, peeled whole
- 4 celery stalks, snapped into thirds, including leaves
- 3 carrots, peeled and snapped in half
- ½ cup fresh parsley, whole with the stems
- Salt to taste

DIRECTIONS:

Add 4 quarts of water to a large stockpot. Add the potatoes, onions, celery, carrots, spinach, and a pinch of salt and pepper to the pot and bring to a boil. After the first hour reduce the heat and simmer for an additional 3 hours. Drain the stock through a sieve into your soup tureen.

BEEF PASTINA SOUP
ZUPPA DI MANZO CON PASTINA

"When I was a young girl, this soup used to deliver two meals for our family. We would enjoy the soup for lunch, and my mother would remove the meat and potatoes and save them for us to have for dinner." - Elisa

SERVES 4-6 PEOPLE

INGREDIENTS:

- 3 pounds beef roast on the bone
- 2 large potatoes, whole and peeled
- 2 large onions, chopped
- 3 celery stalks, chopped
- 3 carrots, chopped
- 1 glove of garlic, chopped
- ¼ cup olive oil
- 8 cups water
- 3 teaspoons salt
- 2 teaspoons black pepper
- ½ pound dry small pasta or pastina

DIRECTIONS:

In a large saucepan, add the olive oil, garlic, and onions and heat until onions start to sizzle. Add the 6 cups of water, beef, potatoes, celery, carrots, salt, and pepper. Simmer for 1½ hours until meat is tender. You may have to add 1-2 cups of additional water. Salt and pepper to taste.

In a separate pot, cook ½ pound of pastina al dente, elbow or your favorite small pasta shape according to package directions. Drain and set aside.

Remove the beef roast and pull apart like strings. Remove the potatoes from the broth and you can discard them since you won't be using them.

To prepare your soup bowls, place ½ cup of pasta in the bowl, add the broth, and top with ½ cup of the beef. Finally, sprinkle grated Parmesan and Romano cheese.

ORZO AND CABBAGE SOUP

ZUPPA D'ORZO E CAPPUCCIO

SERVES 8-10 PEOPLE

INGREDIENTS:

- 16 cups water
- 2 cups carrots, chopped
- 2 yellow onions, chopped
- 3 cups celery, chopped
- 15 ounces canned Cannellini, or white kidney beans
- 4 cups green cabbage, shredded
- 4 cups savoy cabbage, shredded
- ½ cup olive oil
- 3 teaspoons of salt
- 2 teaspoons fresh ground black pepper
- ½ pound of orzo pasta

DIRECTIONS:

In a large stockpot, add the water and olive oil. Chop the carrots, onions, and celery and add them to the pot. Drain the beans and add them to the pot. Finally, shred the cabbage and toss in the pot. Season with salt and pepper and allow to cook for 1½ hours, stirring occasionally. You may have to add some more water if it seems too thick. Add more salt and pepper to taste. Add the orzo, and allow to cook al dente. Remove from heat and serve.

"In the last few years of my husband's life, he started taking fewer and fewer jobs so he could enjoy life more. He even took up golf. I would come home from work and he would be so excited because he had prepared this soup for me. He would make enough to feed us for a week. I miss him everyday, and I have not made this soup since he passed away. This was his dish." - Elisa

CLAM AND POTATO SOUP

ZUPPA DI VONGOLE E PATATE

SERVES 6- 8 PEOPLE

INGREDIENTS

- 2 cups jumbo clams, chopped
- 2 cups potatoes, peeled and cubed, 1-inch by 1-inch
- ⅓ cup celery, sliced
- 2 cups fresh tomatoes, chopped
- 1 large white onion, chopped
- 1 cup carrots, chopped
- ¼ cup fresh oregano, chopped
- ¼ cup fresh parsley, chopped, including the stem
- ¼ cup olive oil
- ¼ cup pancetta or bacon, can be omitted
- 8 cups water
- Salt and pepper to taste
- Fresh Parmesan and Pecorino Romano cheese for garnish, grated

DIRECTIONS

In a large saucepan, add the olive oil, 4 cups of water, and potatoes and allow to boil for 10 minutes, stirring occasionally. Add 1 more cup of water, celery, carrots, tomatoes, onions, and spices and continue to boil for 20 minutes, stirring occasionally. Add the remaining water, clams, and pancetta and boil until the vegetables are tender.

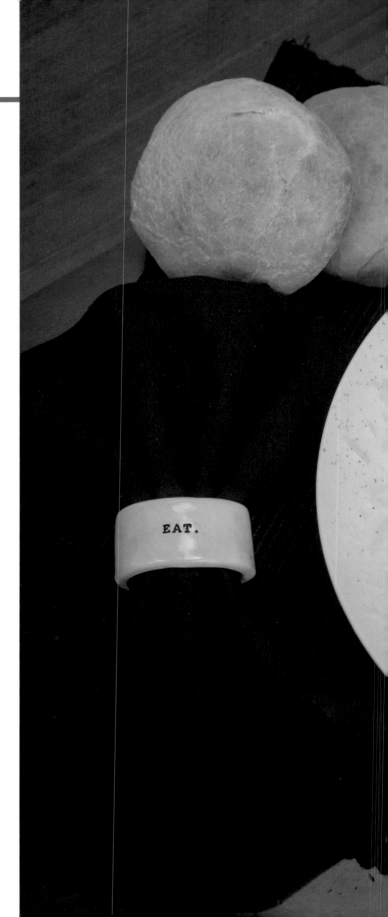

SPLIT PEA SOUP

CREMA DI PISELLI

INGREDIENTS

- 1 cup split peas
- 4 cups water
- 4 beef bouillon cubes
- 2 tablespoons olive oil
- ¼ pound Italian sausage, crumbled
- 1 cup celery, chopped
- 1 large onion, chopped
- 1 garlic clove, chopped
- ½ cup red bell pepper, finely chopped
- ¼ cup red wine
- Salt and fresh black pepper to taste
- ½ cup fresh Parmesan cheese, grated for garnishing

DIRECTIONS

In a large stockpot, combine peas, water, bouillon, and a pinch of salt and pepper and bring to a boil over medium high heat. Once the water begins to boil, reduce the heat and cover. Simmer until the peas are tender, stirring occasionally for about 30 minutes. In a separate skillet, add the olive oil and cook the sausage over medium heat until no longer pink. Add the celery, onion, garlic, and red bell peppers. Sauté for 5 minutes. Add the sausage mixture to the peas along with the wine and simmer for 10-15 minutes uncovered, stirring occasionally. Serve in a soup tureen or individual bowls and garnish with the cheese.

SCRIPPELLE MBUSSE

SERVES 8 PEOPLE

INGREDIENTS

- 24 Scrippelle crêpes,
  see my recipe under Pastas, pg.64
- 2 quarts fresh chicken broth,
  see my recipe under Soups, pg.113
- 1 cup fresh Pecorino Romano
  cheese, grated
- ¼ cup fresh Parmesan cheese,
  shredded
- Fresh parsley for garnishing

DIRECTIONS

Prepare the Scrippelle crêpes and chicken broth according to my recipes. Lay one crêpe at a time on a clean surface and sprinkle the crêpes evenly with the grated Pecorino cheese and roll into tight scrolls. Place 3 crêpes in each serving bowl. Ladle on the boiling broth, garnish with the Parmesan cheese, parsley and serve immediately.

SCRIPPELLE
MBUSSE

LENTIL SOUP

ZUPPA DI LENTICCHIE

SERVES 4-6 PEOPLE

INGREDIENTS:

- 1 ham bone or 3-4 pieces of pork on the bone (optional)
- 1 pound bag dry lentils
- 3 medium onions, finely chopped – set aside ⅓ of the chopped onions
- 2 carrots, peeled and finely chopped
- 3 celery stalks, chopped
- 4 garlic cloves, chopped
- ¼ cup fresh parsley, chopped, including the stem
- 3 large tomatoes, chopped
- Bay leaves, whole
- 1 cup olive oil

DIRECTIONS:

Fill a large stockpot halfway with water and add the lentils and ham bone or pieces of pork and place over medium-high heat. Simmer for 5 minutes and then add ⅔'s of the onions, carrots, celery, garlic, parsley, and 1 bay leaf. Bring to a boil and cook for 1½-2 hours. It is very important that you always maintain a water level above the ingredients, so you may need to add a few cups of water. The lentils are fully cooked when you see them begin to break apart. Reduce the heat and remove the bones.

As the lentils begin to break apart, add the olive oil to a medium sauté pan and heat. Add the remaining third of the onions and the tomatoes and sauté until the onions are soft. Then add the onions and tomatoes to the stockpot and serve. Garnish the center of the bowl of lentils with bay leaves.

MINESTRONE

SERVES 6 PEOPLE

INGREDIENTS:

- 1 pound bag of red kidney beans
- 4 carrots, chopped
- 1 bunch of celery, chopped
- 2 potatoes, peeled and cubed
- 4 onions, chopped & set aside 1 for later
- 2 pounds of escarole, chopped
- 1 cup of olive oil
- 5 large tomatoes, peeled and chopped
- Salt and fresh black pepper to taste
- 1 pound of Ditalini Pasta

DIRECTIONS:

Rinse the beans in a strainer under cold water. Fill a 6-8 quart stockpot with water and place over medium high heat. Add the beans, carrots, potatoes, celery, 3 onions, and escarole and allow to boil for at least one hour. The beans should be tender, and you will notice that they start to break apart. Reduce the heat to a medium low.

Once the beans are cooked, prepare your pasta. In a separate stockpot, bring water to boil and cook the Ditalini al dente. Drain pasta and add beans and vegetables.

While the pasta is cooking, in a medium sauté pan, cook the tomatoes and additional onion with the olive oil for 10-15 minutes and then add to the beans and vegetables. Simmer all together for an additional 10 minutes. Add pasta, stir, and ladle into bowls to serve.

CHICKPEA SOUP

ZUPPA DI CECI

SERVES 4-6 PEOPLE

INGREDIENTS:

- 16 ounces fresh chickpeas, or 3 cans of chickpeas
- 2 Bay leaves, whole
- 1½ cup olive oil
- 3 garlic cloves, whole
- ½ loaf fresh Italian bread
- Salt to taste

DIRECTIONS:

One day before you plan to prepare this soup, soak the chickpeas with 2 teaspoons of salt.

The chickpeas must soak for 24 hours. Canned chickpeas do not need this preparation.

In a medium saucepan, add the soaked chickpeas and water. The water should be roughly 6 inches above the chickpeas. Add the bay leaves, ½ cup of olive oil and garlic and boil for 2½-3 hours. If you are using canned chickpeas, they will only need to boil for 1 hour. Constantly maintain a water level 4-6 inches above the chickpeas.

Cut the bread into 1-inch cubes. In a skillet, heat the remaining cup of olive oil over medium heat and fry the bread cubes. Place the bread cubes in a soup tureen and pour the chickpeas and broth over the bread cubes and serve.

EGG DROP SOUP

ZUPPA DI LENTICCHIE

SERVES 6 PEOPLE

INGREDIENTS:

- 1 quart chicken stock
- 4 eggs, beaten well
- ¼ cup fresh parsley, chopped, including the stems
- Pinch of salt and fresh black pepper
- 1½ tablespoon semolina or all-purpose flour
- 1½ tablespoon fresh Parmesan cheese, grated

OPTIONAL – IN A SEPARATE SAUCEPAN, BOIL ½ POUND OF FRESH SPINACH, CHOP AND ADD TO CHICKEN BROTH AFTER ADDING EGG MIXTURE.

DIRECTIONS:

In a large stockpot, bring the chicken broth to a boil over medium heat. Beat the eggs in a large bowl. Add the flour, cheese, parsley, salt, and pepper and beat until blended thoroughly. Stir the stock in a circular motion. Slowly pour egg mixture into the boiling broth and stir constantly with a large fork; the eggs will form thin strands as it cooks. Continue to stir and simmer for 5 minutes. Add the salt and pepper.

Transfer to bowls or soup tureen. Garnish with additional cheese.

TORTELLINI AND VEGETABLE SOUP

TORTELLINI CON ZUPPA VEGETALE

SERVES 6 PEOPLE

INGREDIENTS:

- 3 carrots, cut into small cubes,
  ½-inch by ½-inch
- 3 celery stalks, sliced lengthwise
  then cut into ½-inch slices
- 8 cups fresh chicken broth,
  see my recipe, in Soups, pg.113
- 1 portion fresh tortellini,
  see my recipe in Pastas, pg.82
  or 1 pound of box tortellini
- 2 ripe tomatoes,
  peeled and chopped
- ¼ cup fresh parsley, chopped,
  including the stem
- ¼ cup fresh Pecorino Romano
  cheese, grated
- 2 tablespoons olive oil
- Pinch of salt and fresh
  black pepper

DIRECTIONS:

In a medium sauté pan, heat the oil, add the carrots and celery and sauté for 5-7 minutes. In a large stockpot, add the chicken broth, parsley, salt, and pepper. Allow broth to simmer over medium heat, add the sautéed carrots, celery, and chopped tomatoes. Bring the broth to a rapid boil and reduce the heat. Drop in the tortellini and cook for 5 minutes, or until they all begin to rise to the top. Ladle into a soup tureen or bowls, garnish with the grated Pecorino cheese, and serve immediately.

ITALIAN WEDDING SOUP

SERVES 8 PEOPLE

"You can serve several simpler versions of this soup by omitting the mini meatballs or omitting both the mini meatballs and escarole. I always ladle 2-3 cups of the chicken broth into a separate saucepan and add just the Scrippelle squares for the children who prefer a simple square soup, as they like to call it." - Elisa

INGREDIENTS

- 24 Scrippelle crêpes, see my recipe under Pastas, pg.64
- 2 quarts fresh chicken broth, see my recipe in this chapter, pg.113
- 3–4 dozen mini meatballs, see my recipe under Meats, pg.146
- 1 pound fresh escarole
- ¼ cup fresh Pecorino Romano or Parmesan cheese, grated

DIRECTIONS

Prepare the Scrippelle crêpes and chicken broth according to my recipes. Bring a separate stockpot of water to a boil and drop in the escarole. Boil the escarole for 20-30 minutes until cooked and soft.

Drain the escarole well, removing all the water and chop finely. Approximately 10 minutes prior to serving, add the escarole to the boiling chicken broth along with the mini meatballs. Line the Scrippelle in a neat pile, and cut into ¼-inch squares. Reduce the heat and drop the cut Scrippelle squares into the broth for 2-3 minutes. Transfer to a soup tureen or ladle into individual bowls. Generously garnish with the grated cheese and serve.

RICE SOUP
ZUPPA DI RISO

SERVES 6-8 PEOPLE

INGREDIENTS

- 4 quarts chicken or vegetable stock, see my recipe in this chapter, pg.113-114
- 2 cups rice
- 1 cup shredded cooked chicken, optional
- ½ cup fresh Pecorino Romano or Parmesan cheese, grated
- 1 cup fresh spinach, boiled and chopped
- Salt to taste

DIRECTIONS

Prepare the rice according to the carton instructions. While the rice is cooking, add the stock to a large stockpot and bring to a boil over medium heat. Add the shredded chicken and spinach and continue to boil for 10-15 minutes. Drain the rice and add to the stock. Add salt to taste. Serve in individual bowls or a soup tureen. Garnish with the grated cheese and serve.

TOMATO MARINARA SAUCE
SUGO AL POMODORO

INGREDIENTS:

- 4 pounds fresh tomatoes or 2 32-ounce cans of crushed tomatoes
- ¾ cup olive oil
- 1 small onion, whole
- 2 garlic cloves, chopped
- 2 celery stalks, finely chopped
- ¼ cup fresh parsley, chopped, including the stem
- 3-4 fresh bay leaves, whole
- Salt and fresh black pepper to taste

DIRECTIONS:

For fresh tomatoes, boil water in a saucepan and add tomatoes. Once the skin begins to wrinkle, remove tomatoes and peel. Allow the tomatoes to cool, and then chop into small pieces.

In a large saucepot, add the oil, onions, garlic and sauté until the onions and garlic have a light golden color. Add the tomatoes, celery, parsley, bay leaves, and some salt and pepper. Bring to a boil, uncovered, over medium heat. Once boiling, reduce the heat and add ¼ cup of water. Continue to simmer for 1½ hours until the sauce thickens.

Remove and season the sauce with more salt and pepper, to taste.

MEAT RAGÙ

"The secret to a wonderful meat Ragù is to include some meat on the bone." – Elisa

INGREDIENTS:

- 8 pounds fresh tomatoes or 4 32-ounce cans of crushed tomatoes
- 2 pounds meat combination, pork, beef, veal, sausage, or ribs
- ½ cup olive oil
- 2 small onions, whole
- 2 garlic cloves, chopped
- 2 celery stalks, finely chopped
- ½ cup fresh parsley, chopped, including the stem
- 3-4 fresh bay leaves, whole
- Salt and fresh black pepper to taste

DIRECTIONS:

For fresh tomatoes, boil water in a saucepan and add tomatoes. Once the skin begins to wrinkle, remove tomatoes and peel. Allow to cool, and chop into small pieces.

In a large saucepot, add the oil, onions, garlic and sauté until the onions and garlic have a light golden color. Add the meats and sauté until the meat browns. Add the tomatoes, celery, parsley, bay leaves, salt and pepper. Bring to a boil, uncovered, over medium heat. Once boiling, reduce the heat and add ¼ cup of water. Continue to simmer for 1½ hours until the sauce thickens. The longer you allow the sauce to cook, the better the flavor.

Remove and season the sauce with salt and pepper, to taste.

"Ragù is characteristically Abruzzese, and refer to any type of meat-based sauce. Ragù is heavily associated with the cooking of Southern Italy as well, and seem to have begun their migration southward from our region." – Elisa

TOMATO SAUCE WITH MEATBALLS
SUGO CON POLPETTE

INGREDIENTS

- 4 pounds fresh tomatoes
  or 2 32-ounce cans of crushed tomatoes
- ¾ cup olive oil
- 1 small onion, whole
- 2 garlic cloves, chopped
- 2 celery stalks, finely chopped
- ¼ cup fresh parsley, chopped,
  including the stem
- 3-4 fresh bay leaves, whole
- 1-1 ½ pound prepared meatballs,
  see my recipe in Meats, pg.146
- Salt and fresh black pepper to taste

DIRECTIONS

For fresh tomatoes, boil water in a saucepan and add tomatoes. Once the skin begins to wrinkle, remove tomatoes and peel. Allow the tomatoes to cool, and chop into small pieces. In a large sauce-pot, add the oil, onions and garlic and sauté for 10 minutes, until the onions and garlic have a light golden color. Add the tomatoes, celery, parsley, bay leaves, and some salt and pepper. Bring to a boil, uncovered over medium heat. Add the meatballs and reduce the heat, and add ¼ cup of water. Continue to simmer for 1 ½ hours until the sauce thickens.

Remove and season the sauce with more salt and pepper, to taste.

WILD SPINACH AND CREAM SAUCE

SPINACI SELVATICI CON SALSA ALLA CREMA

INGREDIENTS:

- 1 pound lean ground beef or veal
- 8 cups fresh wild spinach, chopped
- 1 large yellow onion, chopped
- 2 cups pancetta, diced
- ½ cup carrots, peeled and chopped
- 1½ cups olive oil
- 1 garlic clove, finely chopped
- 1 cup fresh parsley, chopped, including the stem
- 2 cups water
- 3 cups panna or heavy cream
  Parmesan and Romano Pecorino cheese for garnish

DIRECTIONS:

Heat ½ cup of olive oil and the garlic in a large skillet. Once the garlic begins to brown, gradually add the ground meat and pancetta and stir. Allow the ground meat to sauté for 5-10 minutes. Drain the liquid from the pan and return it to the heat. Add ½ cup of water and the onions and carrots. Continue to sauté for 5-10 minutes, stirring occasionally. Add another 1½ cups of water and add the spinach. Lower the heat, cover, and allow to cook for 15 minutes.

In a medium saucepan on low heat, add the heavy cream and parsley and cook until just boiling. Drain any remaining water from the large skillet and add the cream, sauté all together for 2-3 minutes. Remove from the heat and serve over pasta. Garnish with cheese.

"This is a light cream sauce I learned from my mother-in-law when I went to live with my husband's family after we were married. I serve this sauce over fresh Tagliatelle pasta, which you can find under Pastas. You can also serve with boxed penne or rigatoni." – Elisa

BESCIAMELLA SAUCE

SALSA BASCIAMELLA

INGREDIENTS:

- 4 cups whole milk
- 1 stick salted butter
- 2 tablespoons all-purpose flour
- ¼ cup fresh Parmesan cheese, grated
- ¼ cup fresh Pecorino Romano cheese, grated

DIRECTIONS:

In a small saucepan, melt the butter. When melted, stir in the flour to make a smooth paste. Cook, stirring with a wooden spoon for 2-3 minutes. Add the milk, whisking to avoid lumps. Bring to a simmer, whisking until thickened, about 5-7 minutes. Remove from heat, and whisk in the salt and grated cheeses. If the sauce appears too thick, add some milk.

PANCETTA CREAM SAUCE

SALSA ALLA CREMA CON PANCETTA

INGREDIENTS:

- 1 pound of pancetta or bacon, cubed
- 1 stick salted butter
- 2 tablespoons all-purpose flour
- 2 pints heavy cream or panna
- 1 cup fresh Pecorino Romano or Parmesan cheese, grated

DIRECTIONS:

In a medium saucepan, melt the butter over medium heat. Add in the flour and mix well. In a sauté pan, sauté the pancetta for 4-5 minutes, or fry the bacon until cooked. Drain any oil from the pan and add the meat to the butter. Add the heavy cream or panna, cheese and continue to cook over low heat for 5-7 minutes, stirring occasionally.

MEATS

ROASTED LAMB

AGNELLO AL FORNO

SEE PAGE 163

MEATS OF ABRUZZO

My hometown, Poggio Valle, located in the province of Teramo, rose in the Middle Ages. It is a small farming town with an elevation of 983 meters in the Gran Sasso Mountains, which is part of the Appenine chain running through the center of Italy from north to south.

My children assumed that because my family had a farm, we feasted on the livestock we raised. But this was not the case. "Who had meat," I would tell them. We rarely indulged in a second course at mealtime, let alone a meat dish. Animals were raised to be sold in exchange for other household necessities. We only indulged in the slaughtering of our stock for our own consumption on special occasions and holidays. And even then, many families would share the meat of one slaughtered animal and take turns giving up some of their livestock.

For Sunday dinners my father would buy what little meat he could afford, borrowing money to do so most of the time because he believed in having something special on Sundays.

Sometimes my brother would come back from work, and the family he was working for that day was celebrating. They would give him some small cuts of beef or lamb as an extra payment for his excellent work; my mother would use this meat to prepare the most wonderful stews, which I share with you in these pages.

The slaughtering of animals was the responsibility of the men, and the busiest times of the year were in January and at Easter. Although it was not very easy to travel to my town, most people walked, rode horses or those more fortunate came by motorbike. In January, my town had many visitors willing to make the long and treacherous journey looking to purchase fresh pork, an omnipresent meat staple in Italy. They would partake in the annual tradition of preparing sausages as well as smoked and cured meat products such as soppressata and prosciutto.

Most families would prepare dried sausage for the upcoming months, but also (and more famous in my region) they would press large pieces of fat, lean pork and some liver, and season it with nutmeg, spices, and garlic. Then it would be sealed in jars, and served as lunch spread on fresh bread for those working in the fields or as a late afternoon snack called a 'merenda'. These jars would last throughout the summer and into the autumn months.

Mortadella is another famous product from my region; it is a small cured meat, with a longish oval-shape. Inside, it is dark red, with a white column of fat. They are generally sold two tied together. They are about as big as two cupped hands put together. Another name for the Mortadella in Italian is "coglioni di mulo" (donkey's balls).

Although our pork is considered among the very best in Italy, our lamb's superiority is uncontested. It's superiority was credited to the animals' mountain-grazed diets rich in herbs. The steep mountains in part of the countryside lend themselves well to sheep and goat herding. And the weeks leading up to Easter brought many repeat customers for fresh lamb. Chicken, turkey and wild fowl are also plentiful on the farms in my town and were also sold in exchange for goods.

As the men dealt with the visitors searching for the best meats, the women provided these visitors with plenty of fresh parsley, rosemary, garlic, and olive oil—all of which hold a prominent place in the flavoring of dishes from my region.

The most flavorful local recipes started out as necessity, ways to use readily available ingredients and leftovers to produce food that was both practical and pleasant. Almost every edible part of livestock is utilized somehow in Abruzzese cooking. Nothing is wasted, and little is lost. The people are frugal, but hearty. Today's Abruzzese dishes hold true to the past and marry earthy flavors with spices to make the palate sing. Isn't that what we really want from Italian food? It is how I have prepared meals for my family and friends for decades.

ROASTED CHICKEN
POLLO SPEZZATO AL FORNO

SEE PAGE 162

CHICKEN & MUSHROOM MARSALA

POLLO E FUNGHI ALLA MARSALA

SERVES 8–10 PEOPLE

INGREDIENTS:

- 8 cups chicken breast, uncooked and cubed
- 4 cups fresh mushrooms, sliced
- ¼ cup celery, chopped
- ½ cup white onion, chopped
- ½ cup all-purpose flour
- 1 cup whole milk
- ½ cup heavy cream
- ½ cup Marsala Wine
- 4 fresh basil leaves
- ¼ cup mayonnaise
- 2 cups fresh Parmesan cheese, grated
- ½ cup Italian-style bread crumbs

DIRECTIONS:

Preheat oven to 350 degrees F.

In a large mixing bowl, whisk the milk, heavy cream, mayonnaise, and basil leaves. Sift the flour into the milk mixture and beat thoroughly.

Place the chicken, mushrooms, celery, and onion in a separate large bowl, and toss well. Add the milk mixture to this bowl and mix with a wooden spoon. Pour these ingredients into a 13 x 9 x 2-inch glass casserole pan. Pour wine evenly over the dish. Sprinkle the cheese evenly over the mixture, then repeat with the breadcrumbs.

Place in the oven and bake until the top is golden brown and crispy, roughly 30 minutes depending on the oven.

BEEF STEW

SPEZZATO DI MANZO

SERVES 6–8 PEOPLE

"There is nothing more comforting than a delicious stew. This is one of the first dishes my mother taught me to make. Serve with some fresh baked bread or fried dough." – Elisa

INGREDIENTS:

- 3 pounds Choice Beef Chuck (or another tender cut of beef), cubed
- 6 Idaho potatoes, peeled and cubed
- 3 onions, chopped
- 2 garlic cloves, chopped
- ½ cup of Pinot Grigio, or homemade Italian white wine
- 4 cups carrots, sliced into ½-inch slices
- 4 cups celery, sliced into ½-inch pieces
- ½ cup fresh parsley, chopped, include the stalks
- 2 tablespoons salt
- 1 teaspoon fresh black pepper
- ½ cup cornstarch
- 1 teaspoon butter, melted
- ¼ cup olive oil
- 1 cup fresh Pecorino Romano or Parmesan cheese, grated

DIRECTIONS:

In a large stockpot, add olive oil, onions, garlic, and beef and let cook for 5 minutes. Next add the white wine, salt, and pepper and continue to simmer for 1 hour, mixing occasionally. Add ½ cup of water, if needed, to prevent drying out the meat. Add the carrots, celery, parsley, and continue to simmer for 20 minutes.

Give the stew a good stir and add 2 more cups of water to the pot. Drop in the potatoes and cook for the final 30 minutes, stirring occasionally. In a small bowl, beat the cornstarch, butter, a pinch of fresh pepper and a cup of the juices from the stew. Beat until there are no lumps and pour back into the stew pot. You could also use a pouch of brown gravy mix instead. Remove from heat and serve.

CHICKEN BREAST STUFFED WITH PROSCIUTTO

PETTO DI POLLO RIPIENO CON PROSCIUTTO

"I created this dish in the mid-90s while my son was away at college. He would always be bored with the same old dinners when he came home, so I created this and serve it with my rice and onions and sautéed zucchini. It is called 'Frankie's Chicken'." - Elisa

INGREDIENTS:

- 4-6 chicken breasts
- 3 cups Italian bread crumbs
- ½ cup olive oil
- ¾ pound fresh mozzarella cheese, shredded
- 2 garlic cloves, chopped
- 2 teaspoons crushed red pepper
- ½ cup fresh parsley, chopped, including the stalk
- 1 teaspoon black pepper
- 2 teaspoons salt
- 4-5 slices prosciutto, or 3 mild or homemade Italian sausage links, chopped
- 3 cups chicken stock, see my recipe under Soups, pg.113

DIRECTIONS:

Preheat oven to 350 degrees F.

Pour 1 cup of the chicken stock in a small glass bowl. Trim all fat from the chicken breasts and slice down the center. Tenderize with mallet, dip in the bowl of chicken stock, and set aside on a plate.

Prepare the filling in a large glass bowl; combine 2 cups of the breadcrumbs, olive oil, cheese, garlic, red pepper, parsley and prosciutto or sausage. Mix well with your hands. Add the salt and pepper. The mixture should be moist. If you think it is dry, add a few teaspoons of water. Spread the filling evenly over the open chicken breasts with a spatula. Give a firm press with your fingertips. Start on one side of the chicken breast and roll. Use 2-3 toothpicks per breast to secure them.

Place the chicken breast in a small roasting pan or 13 x 9 x 2-inch glass baking pan. Pour the 2 cups of chicken stock and two cups of water into the pan covering the chicken breast halfway with the liquid. Sprinkle the remaining breadcrumbs over the top of the chicken breasts with a pinch of salt and black pepper.

Place in the oven and bake for 45 minutes. Baste the chicken every 10 minutes with the juices from the pan to keep them from drying out. You can always add more chicken stock if needed. Remove from oven and serve, pouring the juices over the chicken breasts.

SCALOPPINI

SERVES 4-6 PEOPLE

INGREDIENTS:

- 3 pounds lamb, veal or chicken, cut into 1- inch by 1-inch pieces
- 2 large white onions, chopped
- 2 garlic cloves, chopped
- ¼ cup fresh parsley, chopped, including the stems
- 2 red peppers, sliced
- 2 green peppers, sliced
- 1 yellow pepper, sliced
- 1 cup olive oil
- ½ cup dry white wine or cooking wine
- 4–6 large tomatoes, diced or 1 28 ounce can of crushed tomatoes
- 2 teaspoons fresh black pepper
- 2 teaspoons salt

DIRECTIONS:

In a medium saucepan, add the olive oil and heat for 2-3 minutes. Add the onions, garlic, and parsley and simmer for 5 minutes. Add the meat and white wine. Stir for 2-3 minutes as meat starts to cook. Add the peppers and fry together for 10 minutes.

Add the tomatoes and simmer on medium heat for 45 minutes to 1 hour depending on the tenderness of the meat. Remove from heat, and place in a serving bowl. Garnish with grated Parmesan and Romano cheese and parsley.

" In Abruzzo, scaloppini was traditionally made with lamb. However you can substitute the lamb with veal or chicken." - Elisa

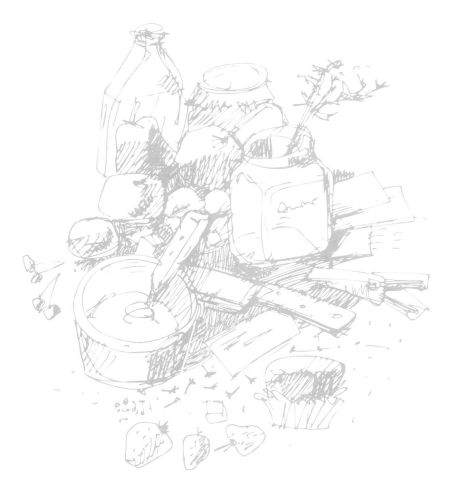

WILD BOAR
CINGHIALE

INGREDIENTS:

- 3 pounds wild boar, cut into pieces
- 2 white onions, sliced
- 1 cup butter
- 2 carrots, chopped
- 3 celery stalks, sliced, ¼ inch thick
- 2 garlic cloves, sliced
- ½ cup olive oil
- 2 tablespoons salt
- 1 tablespoon fresh black pepper
- 2 cups dry white wine
- Water for boiling

DIRECTIONS:

Fill a large saucepan with water and bring to a boil. Wash the meat and cut into pieces. Place the meat into the boiling water and add the salt. Strain the meat out of the water, place in a bowl, and ladle enough water from the saucepan to cover the meat; set aside. Do not discard the boiled water yet.

In a large skillet, melt the butter and add the carrots, celery, onions and garlic; sauté for 5 minutes. Add the wine and 1 cup of water from the saucepan, lower the heat and simmer, mixing occasionally. Add the boar to the skillet, with a pinch of salt and black pepper, and cook until meat is brown. Remove from heat and place in serving bowl.

CHICKEN WITH SAUSAGE, PEPPERS AND OLIVES

POLLO CON SALSICCIA, PEPERONI E OLIVE

SERVES 6 PEOPLE

INGREDIENTS:

- 1 3½-4 pound whole roasting chicken
- 1 pound hot Italian Sausage, sliced
- 2 cups sweet green peppers, chopped
- 1 cup white onion, chopped
- 1 garlic clove, finely chopped
- 2 cups fresh tomatoes, chopped
- 1 cup chicken stock
- 1 cup pitted black olives
- 2 tablespoons all-purpose flour
- 1 tablespoon olive oil

DIRECTIONS:

Cut up the chicken into pieces for frying. In a large skillet or Dutch oven with a lid, add the oil and brown the chicken for 10-15 minutes. Remove the chicken with tongs, place in a bowl, and set aside.

Without rinsing the pan, cook the sausages until they are lightly browned. Remove them and dry on a paper towel-covered plate.

Drain all but 2 tablespoons of the fat from the pan. Add the peppers, onions and garlic to the pan and sauté for 5 minutes. Stir in the flour. Gradually add the chicken broth, stirring constantly. Return the sausage and chicken to the pot and add the tomatoes and olives. Cover and cook on low heat for 45 minutes or until the chicken is tender.

"This recipe has been shared with me by my dear friend and co-worker, Teresa Mancini." - Elisa

BRACIOLE

SERVES 4-6 PEOPLE

INGREDIENTS

- 2 pounds of whole flank steak, cut into 3 portions, then slice in half
- ½ cup fresh parsley, chopped, including stems
- ¼ cup fresh oregano, chopped
- 4 garlic cloves, chopped
- ¼ cup olive oil
- ½ cup Italian-style bread crumbs
- ½ cup fresh Pecorino Romano cheese, grated
- ½ cup fresh Parmesan cheese, grated
- 1 cup fresh mozzarella cheese (whole), cut in pinky-sized slices
- 2 teaspoons salt
- 1 teaspoon fresh black pepper
- ½ cup red wine
- Baker's twine
- 4 cups tomato sauce, see my recipe in Sauces, pg.126

DIRECTIONS

Using a meat mallet, tenderize the flank steak. Place olive oil in a medium bowl, dip each piece of flank steak into the oil, and place on a clean surface. In a separate medium-sized bowl, combine the garlic, breadcrumbs, parsley, oregano, Pecorino Romano, Parmesan, oil, salt, and pepper. Using your hands, mix thoroughly.

Place a strip of mozzarella cheese onto each piece of flank steak, and then evenly divide the stuffing mixture over each piece of flank steak. Roll each piece of flank steak lengthwise and secure with twine in the center and ¼-inch from both ends.

Using a medium saucepan with a lid, heat the wine and ½ cup of water on medium-high heat. Place bracioles into liquid carefully and continue turning to brown on all sides for about 6-8 minutes. Once browned, pour in the sauce, reduce to low heat; and let cook slowly for 2 hours. Remove from heat and serve as antipasto or with your favorite vegetables and a nice salad.

TRIPE

TRIPPA FIORENTINA

INGREDIENTS:

- 2 pounds tripe
- ½ cup olive oil
- 2 garlic cloves, chopped
- 2 celery stalks, chopped
- 2 carrots, chopped
- 1 large onion, chopped
- 2 cups fresh parsley, chopped, including the stems
- 8 cups fresh tomatoes, chopped
- Salt and freshly ground black pepper
- ½ cup Parmesan cheese, grated
- ½ cup Pecorino Romano cheese, grated

DIRECTIONS:

Fill a large stockpot with water and bring to boil. Add the tripe and 2 teaspoons of salt and allow the tripe to boil for 1 hour. After 1 hour, remove the tripe and cut into pieces approximately 2 inches wide by 2 inches long.

Set aside while you prepare the skillet.

In a large skillet, heat the oil and garlic. Add the celery, carrots, onion, parsley, and sauté for 20 minutes. Next add the cut tripe to the skillet and continue to sauté for an additional 40 minutes.

Transfer the contents in the skillet to a medium saucepan and add the tomatoes and a pinch of black pepper. Cook for 45 minutes stirring occasionally. Transfer to a serving platter and garnish with the cheese.

"When it came time to slaughter animals, many families utilized every part of the animal to provide a meal, including stomachs. We would also prepare this dish when we were having guests for dinner and sometimes served it as an antipasto." - Elisa

THREE CHEESE "MEATLESS" MEATBALLS

POLPETTE DI FORMAGGIO

INGREDIENTS

- 1 pound ricotta cheese, drained
- 1½ cups fresh Parmesan and Pecorino Romano, grated
- 1½ cups Italian breadcrumbs
- ¼ cup fresh Italian parsley, chopped, include the stem
- ¼ teaspoon salt
- ¼ cup vegetable oil, for frying

DIRECTIONS

Preheat the oil in a large frying pan.

Combine the ricotta, Parmesan, Pecorino Romano, parsley, and breadcrumbs and mix together with your hands. Form into the size of golf balls and place 3-5 at a time in the heated oil. Fry the balls until brown on all sides. Remove and dry on a paper towel. Add to sauce when ready.

LAMB STEW

SPEZZATO DI AGNELLO

SERVES 4–6 PEOPLE

INGREDIENTS

- 2½ pound lamb, cut into 1-inch cubes
- 1 pound rustic potatoes, peeled and sliced
- ¼ cup fresh Parmesan cheese, diced
- 2 ounces Pecorino Romano cheese, grated or shredded
- ½ cup red wine
- 3 garlic cloves, chopped
- 2 tablespoons Crisco or butter
- 1 large onion, chopped
- ½ cup olive oil
- Salt and fresh black pepper to taste

DIRECTIONS

Add the olive oil and onions to a medium saucepan and sauté over medium high heat. Once the onions become translucent, add the Crisco or butter and allow to melt. Once melted, add the lamb pieces, parsley, garlic and a pinch or two of salt. Sauté the lamb until it is well browned, then add the red wine. Continue to cook until all the wine has evaporated. Add the potatoes and enough warm water to cover all the ingredients. Place a lid on the pot and simmer for about 40 minutes or until the lamb is tender. Remove from heat and add diced Parmesan and mix thoroughly. Transfer the stew to a serving dish and garnish with the Pecorino Romano before serving.

GRILLED LAMB SKEWERS
ARROSTICINI

MAKES ABOUT 3 DOZEN SKEWERS

INGREDIENTS:

- 3 pounds mutton or lamb
- ½ cup olive oil
- Fresh rosemary
- Salt and fresh black pepper
- Wooden skewers

DIRECTIONS:

Soak the wooden skewers in a bath of cold water for 1 hour.

Trim all the fat and cut the meat into very small pieces or ½-inch cubes. Thread the meat onto the skewers, up to 1-inch from the top. There should be 5 inches of meat on each skewer.

Line the skewers on a cookie sheet with the handle parts of the skewers hanging off the cookie sheet, and pour the olive oil over the meat. Garnish with some salt, pepper, and fresh rosemary and allow to marinate for 1 hour in the refrigerator.

Remove the skewers from the refrigerator and place on a brazier and cook on the grill for 10 minutes, 5 minutes on each side. Brush the skewers with fresh rosemary stalk dipped in olive oil while cooking and salt to taste. Remove from the grill and serve.

"This dish is a traditional part of our Sunday BBQ and local festivals, and is usually made with sheep (mutton) meat and cooked on a brazier. They are one of the most recognizable symbols of the Teramo Province's cuisine. My husband built our family a grill especially for this traditional favorite. My grandchildren call these skewers 'meat on a stick'." - Elisa

GRILLED
LAMB
SKEWERS
ARROSTICINI

MY MEATBALL STORY

When most people think of Italian meatballs they envision big round mounds of meat. They may imagine veal, pork, and beef packed together in snowball-sized concoctions that are first fried to a golden brown on the exterior and left to simmer in sauce to complete the cooking. Most Italian-Americans serve meatballs atop spaghetti or other long pasta noodles.

This all sounds perfectly wonderful, but I must admit … this is the furthest thing from my thoughts when I think of meatballs.

In my experience, meatballs are something quite different altogether: small and pea-sized, added to soups on special occasions or mixed with sauce and tossed with pasta. The way I have always prepared meatballs is in keeping with a mindset that informs how a lot of Italian recipes came to life. You must remember that I grew up and learned to cook in a time before refrigeration, in a rural town far removed from stores and markets, and under a belief that we should use every ingredient to its fullest extent possible.

So, when we were tasked to prepare meatballs, it was because we were using fresh ingredients to breathe new life into those that had been preserved. Our supplies were limited, and therefore, precious. Ingredients had to be handled with care, and they had to be made to last without the use of refrigeration.

Meatballs are the perfect example of this. When we got access to meat, such as when a cow or pig was slaughtered or when a merchant arrived in our village, we may have cooked the best parts for a meal, but we also saved some to make sausages that could hang to dry so they could last for months after. We could then cook those sausages in future meals, or, if the occasion called for it, split them open and use the meat to make meatballs, which we would add to freshly prepared sauces and soups.

I have many memories of making pallottine, miniature meatballs for soup or timballo, a sort of lasagna made with scrippelle (crêpes) instead of pasta. Of course, when I cooked under the tutelage of Zia Ida, we made pallottine many times for traditional wedding soup. But I recall another story about these little meatballs that also involved dancing and a certain young man, where I got into a fair amount of trouble …

Making proper pallottine is a fairly labor intensive process. They are made in a way that is similar to most meatball recipes, using meat, eggs, breadcrumbs, and usually grated cheese.

But, owing to their smaller size, it can take longer to make and shape an entire batch. On one occasion when I could not have been much older than fifteen, my brother Joe and I were tasked to make pallottine for our family dinner the following day. I remember this well because, tragically, we were still in the year of mourning after our sister Dorina had passed away while in childbirth.

We were meant to be solemn and serious during this year. But Joe had other plans. There was a fabulous party being held in the town square, and we could hear the music and laughter as our friends were dancing the night away. Joe knew how much I loved to dance, so he told me to work fast and finish the batch of meatballs so we could sneak away.

After we had prepared the pallottine, Joe and I snuck away to the dance. We shed the traditional black clothes we were supposed to be wearing in remembrance of our sister to put on clothing more befitting the occasion. Oh what a time we had! It was great fun, and that night, I just happened to catch the eye of a young boy who would later play an important role in my life, and no it was not my future husband. That story will come later.

I am sure you know how this story would end, of course. Joe and I were not as clever as we thought, and our older brother, Vincenzo, caught us as we were sneaking back into our rooms and got very angry with us. My parents were also very angry, and they punished me for months after for having shirked my duties and for disgracing my family to go dancing.

I have not made pallottine 'mini meatballs' regularly since 1981. I was preparing them when I learned my daughter Agnes had taken a turn for the worse in the hospital, and it would be the beginning of one of the worse nightmares any mother could endure, the loss of a child.

Although pallottine has shared its place at many holiday celebrations, it is also associated with memories of loved ones I have lost. And so, making meatballs has a bittersweet association in my mind.

When I think of pallottine, I am filled with a sense of longing to be in the company again of cherished loved ones no longer here. And yet, pallottine, and how they are made, is a useful reminder of life: in the same way we use fresh ingredients to breathe new life into those that are preserved, the love we share with those still around us can help us remember the love we shared with those no longer with us but whose memories we hold and cherish dear in our hearts.

LITTLE MEATBALLS

POLPOTTINE

MAKES APPROXIMATELY 3 DOZEN MEATBALLS

INGREDIENTS:

- 2 eggs
- ½ teaspoon salt
- 1 pound lean ground beef
- ¼ cup Italian breadcrumbs
- ½ cup fresh Parmesan or Pecorino Romano, grated
- ¼ cup olive oil

DIRECTIONS:

Preheat the olive oil in a large frying pan.

Beat the eggs in a glass mixing bowl. Add the beef, salt, breadcrumbs, and cheese and mix together with your hands. Roll each meatball into tiny balls, as small as possible, the size of a chickpea.

When the oil is hot, add the meatballs, in small amounts and fry until brown on all sides. Remove and dry on a paper towel-covered plate. Set aside for when you are ready to add them to your lasagna or soups.

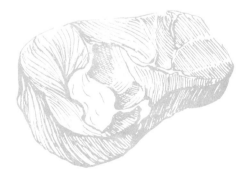

"These are the meatballs I use for my lasagnas and for my soups. As this was my task growing up, it also became my daughter Nadia's task when helping me in the kitchen. You can also use these to garnish a bowl of spaghetti, the way they were traditionally served." - Elisa

MEATBALLS
POLPETTE

MAKES ABOUT 12 MEATBALLS

"I believe many chefs and cooks try to overdo this simple dish. I have used this recipe for years and my guests are always very pleased. It is one of my most requested recipes from friends and family." - Elisa

INGREDIENTS

- 2 eggs
- 1 pound ground beef
- 1 cup water
- ¼ cup fresh Italian parsley, chopped, include the stalks
- 1 cup Italian-style breadcrumbs
- 2 garlic cloves, chopped
- ½ teaspoon salt
- ¼ cup Parmesan or Pecorino Romano cheese, grated

DIRECTIONS

Preheat oven to 350 degrees F.

Beat the eggs in a glass mixing bowl. Add the beef, parsley, breadcrumbs, garlic, salt, and cheese and mix all together with your hands. Gradually add in the water and continue to mix.

Roll each meatball into the size of a golf ball. Place in a baking pan 1-inch apart and bake for 30-40 minutes. Remove meatballs and place on wire rack and allow to cool for at least 15-20 minutes. Add to sauce when ready.

BEEF MEATLOAF
POLPETTONE DI MANZO

SERVES 6-8 PEOPLE

INGREDIENTS:

- 1½ pounds lean ground beef
- 2 eggs
- ½ cup water
- ½ cup white onion, chopped
- 2 cloves garlic, chopped
- ½ cup breadcrumbs
- ¼ cup fresh Italian parsley, chopped, include the stalk
- ½-1 teaspoon salt
- ¼ cup olive oil
- 2 tablespoons red wine

DIRECTIONS:

Preheat oven to 350 degrees F.

Beat the eggs in a large mixing bowl. Add the beef, parsley, onions, garlic, salt, and breadcrumbs and mix together with your hands. Gradually add in the water and continue to mix.

Using a large loaf pan or 2 small loaf pans, grease the pans with the olive oil and wine. Form the mixture into the pans and bake for 1 hour depending on your oven. Remove once top has browned.

POT ROAST
MANZO ALLA GENOVESE

SERVES 8-10 PEOPLE

INGREDIENTS:

- 4 pounds Eye Round Roast
- 1 large onion, sliced
- 3 celery stalks, cut into thirds
- 3 carrots, peeled and cut into thirds
- 4 garlic cloves, whole
- ¼ cup fresh rosemary
- 1 cup dry white wine
- 1 cup olive oil
- 4 cups water to start
- Salt and fresh black pepper to taste

DIRECTIONS:

In a large stockpot, add the olive oil and round roast. Brown the meat on all sides on medium to low heat, turning regularly for 30 minutes. While the roast is browning, prepare your vegetables.

Add the onion, celery, carrots, garlic, rosemary, and a pinch of salt and pepper to the pot. Add the 4 cups of water and the wine to the pot. Cover the pot, leaving a small opening and simmer for 2½-3 hours. As the water reduces, continue to add water to prevent burning.

Remove the meat and slice into ½-inch slices. Place the slices on a serving dish. Puree the vegetables and remaining juices from the pot for 2 minutes, pour over the meat and serve.

VENISON STEW
STUFATO DI CERVO

SERVES 4 PEOPLE

INGREDIENTS:

- 4 pounds venison, cubed for stewing
- 3 garlic cloves, chopped
- 2 onions, chopped
- ½ cup fresh parsley, chopped including the stem
- ½ cup celery, chopped
- ½ cup olive oil
- 1 cup dry white wine
- 1 28-ounce can of crushed tomatoes
- 3 cups water
- 3 teaspoons salt
- Fresh black pepper to taste

DIRECTIONS:

Soak the venison cubes in a bath of cold water and the salt in a glass mixing bowl for 24 hours in the refrigerator. Remove the venison from the refrigerator and rinse under cold water and place in a large sauté pan over medium heat. Sauté for 10-15 minutes. Drain the water that sweats from the meat. Return the pan to the stovetop and reduce the heat to medium low.

Add the water, wine, olive oil, celery, parsley, onions, and garlic and sauté for 45 minutes.

Next add the crushed tomatoes and continue to simmer for an additional 30 minutes. Remove from heat and serve with fresh Italian bread to help soak up the gravy.

" I have adjusted and perfected this recipe over the years. Although venison can be difficult to find in local grocery stores, we all have hunters in our lives who love to share the wealth of their hunt. In my case it is my brother Nicola, who fills my freezer every year with this delicious treat." - Elisa

ITALIAN ROADSIDE ROAST PORK

PORCHETTA ABRUZZESE

SERVES 6-8 PEOPLE

INGREDIENTS:

- 1 4-6 lb. pork hip or shoulder, with skin if available
- 8 garlic cloves
- ¼ cup olive oil
- ½ cup dry white wine
- ½ cup fresh rosemary
- Salt and fresh black pepper to taste

DIRECTIONS:

Preheat oven to 350 degrees F.

Grease a roasting pan with some olive oil and add the pork hip. Take a knife and make 8-10 small incisions 2-inches deep. Insert the garlic cloves without peeling them. Insert some rosemary into the incisions as well. Pour the wine and olive oil over the meat. Add salt and pepper to taste and garnish with remaining rosemary. Add a cup of water to the pan as well. Roast in the oven for about one hour to 90 minutes or until the center of the pork is no longer pink. The pork should be basted frequently with the drippings from the pan.

Remove from the oven and allow to cool for 15 minutes before serving. Garnish with the drippings from the pan. Also may be served as sandwiches with fresh Italian hard rolls.

" Since the 15th century the people in my region have prepared suckling pig. If you visit Abruzzo, you will surely come in contact with porchetta trucks that travel throughout the region, setting up shop in piazzas, outdoor markets, festivals, and by the roadside. You can buy the meat, sliced to order from a freshly roasted pig, to take home or grab a Panini to go. The sandwiches are filled with thin slices of porchetta that have been perfectly seasoned and served with the best of breads. My favorite part is the crunchy skin." - Elisa

ITALIAN
ROADSIDE
ROAST PORK
———
PORCHETTA
ABRUZZESE

PAN-ROASTED QUAIL

QUAGLIE AL DECAME

SERVES 4-6 PEOPLE

"There are two ways I like to prepare quail. The first is roasting them whole with some stuffing for added flavor. The other is the way my husband preferred them, pan-roasted. I would cook six quails and he would eat them all. He loved this dish and I miss having the opportunity to prepare them for him. You can also prepare Cornish hens with this recipe." - Elisa

INGREDIENTS

- 4–6 fresh whole quail, rinsed
- ¼ cup fresh rosemary
- 2 garlic cloves, chopped
- 2 cups dry white wine
- ½ cup olive oil
- Salt and fresh black pepper to taste
- ¼ cup Italian sausage, crumbed
- 2 cups Italian bread, chopped into small pieces
- 2 tablespoons chicken broth
- ¼ cup celery, finely chopped
- ¼ cup onion, finely chopped

DIRECTIONS

In the Oven:

Preheat oven to 350 degrees F.

If you are preparing stuffing:

Wash and rinse the quail under cold water and set aside on a paper towel. In a large glass bowl, combine the rosemary, garlic, wine, and olive oil. Drop the quail into the mixture and turn so the quail is completely coated. Place the quail in a glass casserole dish, breast side up. Add a pinch of salt and pepper.

If you plan on stuffing the quail, which is optional—some people prefer not to stuff their roasted birds—combine all the ingredients for the stuffing in a bowl and mix well with your hands. Using a teaspoon, stuff each quail with the stuffing. Add 1 cup of water to the pan, cover loosely with aluminum foil and place in the oven. Bake for 20 minutes, basting occasionally. Remove the foil and bake for an additional 15-20 minutes. Be careful that the quail does not dry out. Remove from the oven and serve.

On the Stovetop:

Wash and rinse the quail under cold water and set aside on a paper towel. Combine the rosemary, garlic, wine, 1 cup of water, and olive oil in a large sauté pan with a lid. Using kitchen scissors cut the quail into pieces, separating the limbs and splitting the breast. Drop the quail pieces into the pan, and mix thoroughly until the quail is completely coated. Cover and simmer over medium heat for 1 hour, stirring occasionally. Add a pinch of salt and pepper.

You can remove the lid after 40 minutes, and add a little water to the pan to avoid the quail sticking to the pan. Remove from the heat, and transfer to a serving bowl. Serve with my roasted potatoes for a delicious meal and think of my husband, as this was one of his favorite dinners.

ROASTED RABBIT

CONIGLIO ARROSTO

SERVES 4 PEOPLE

INGREDIENTS:

- 1 whole rabbit, cleaned and cut into parts
- ½ cup fresh parsley, chopped, including the stem
- ¼ cup fresh oregano, chopped
- 2 tablespoons fresh rosemary
- 4 garlic cloves, chopped
- 1 cup olive oil
- 2 cups dry white wine
- 2 teaspoons salt
- 1 teaspoon black pepper

DIRECTIONS:

Preheat to 375 degrees F.

Rinse the rabbit under cold water and chop into pieces. In a large bowl, combine the olive oil, herbs, garlic, salt, and pepper. Drop each piece of the rabbit into the mixture and coat; transfer the pieces to a roasting pan.

Pour the wine over the rabbit and add another pinch or two of salt.

Cook uncovered for 1 hour, basting occasionally with the wine. Remove from oven and transfer to a serving platter. Drizzle the remaining juices from the pan over the roasted rabbit pieces and serve.

ROAST LEG OF LAMB

AGNELLINO AL FORNO

SERVES 6 PEOPLE

INGREDIENTS:

- 3-4 pounds leg of lamb
- 6 garlic cloves, finely chopped
- ½ cup fresh rosemary
- 1 cup olive oil
- ½ cup of fresh parsley, chopped, including the stem
- 1 cup dry white wine
- Pinch of salt and fresh black pepper

DIRECTIONS:

Preheat oven to 375 degrees F.

Rinse and wipe the leg of lamb. With the point of a sharp knife make small incisions all over the surface. Place the lamb in a roasting pan. Combine the wine, olive oil, rosemary, parsley, salt, and pepper in a bowl and beat well. Pour the mixture into the incisions and over the top of the meat.

Cook the lamb for 30-45 minutes, basting occasionally with the pan juices.

ITALIAN-STYLE FRIED CHICKEN

POLLO FRITTO ALL ' ITALIANA

SERVES 4-6 PEOPLE

INGREDIENTS:

- 2 pounds chicken, drumsticks, breasts, and wings
- 1 cup flour
- 1 tablespoon garlic powder
- 2 eggs
- ½ teaspoon salt
- ¼ teaspoon fresh black pepper
- 2 cups vegetable oil, for frying

DIRECTIONS:

Preheat oven to 350 degrees F.

Rinse the chicken pieces under cold water and pat dry. Combine the flour, garlic powder, salt, and pepper in a bowl. In a separate bowl beat the eggs. Dip the chicken pieces one-by-one into the eggs, then roll in the flour.

Heat the oil in a deep skillet over medium heat. Fry the chicken a few pieces at a time until golden brown; turn the chicken for even frying. Drain the chicken on a paper towel and place the chicken on a baking sheet. Bake for 30-40 minutes or until the juices run clear when pierced with a knife. Remove from the oven and transfer to a serving platter.

CHICKEN WITH EGGPLANT

SPEZZATO DI POLLO CON MELANZANE

SERVES 4-6 PEOPLE

INGREDIENTS:

- 1 Roasting Chicken
- 5 eggplants
- 1 cup olive oil
- 2 garlic cloves, crushed
- 1 cup dry white wine
- 1 pound fresh tomatoes
- ¼ pound of bacon, chopped
- ½ cup of fresh parsley, chopped, including the stem
- Salt and fresh black pepper to taste

DIRECTIONS:

Wash the chicken under cold water. Chop the chicken into pieces, separating the legs, wings, and thighs. Peel and chop the eggplants into small pieces. Place in a colander and add the salt. Toss and allow to sit for 1 hour to drain their juices.

In a large sauté pan, heat ⅓ of the olive oil, add the garlic, and sauté until it is lightly brown. Add the chicken pieces to the pan and fry them on all sides until they are golden brown. Add a pinch of salt and pepper and add the wine. Cook the chicken until the wine has evaporated.

Peel and chop the tomatoes, removing the seeds, and add to the pan as soon as the wine has evaporated. Add ½ cup of water and the bacon. Cover and cook over medium low heat for 30 minutes. Check that the pan maintains some water at all times, adding water if needed.

In a separate sauté pan, add the remaining olive oil, eggplant, some pepper and the parsley and sauté the eggplant over medium heat for 15 minutes.

Transfer the chicken to a serving platter, pour the eggplant over the chicken, and serve.

ROASTED PORK CHOPS

BRACIOLE DI MAIALE

SERVES 6-8 PEOPLE

INGREDIENTS:

- 6-8 center cut, bone-in Pork chops
- ½ cup olive oil
- ½ cup dry white wine
- 1 tablespoon salt
- 1 tablespoon fresh black pepper
- ¼ cup fresh rosemary
- 2 garlic cloves, finely chopped

DIRECTIONS:

Preheat oven to 400 degrees F.

Rinse the pork chops under cold water and set aside. In a glass mixing bowl large enough to hold all the pork chops, add the olive oil, wine, salt, pepper, and garlic and beat with a fork to blend all the ingredients.

Tenderize the pork chops with a meat tenderizer on both sides. Soak both sides of the chops in the mixture. Line the pork chops in a roasting pan and pour the remaining mixture over the meat and place in a refrigerator for 20 minutes.

Remove the pork chops from the refrigerator and place a large skillet over medium heat. Place the pork chops in the skillet and sear for 3-4 minutes on each side.

Return the pork chops to the roasting pan and sprinkle the rosemary over the tops of the pork chops. Add a splash of water and some wine to the pan and place them in the oven and cook for 20 minutes.

Remove the pork chops from the oven and arrange on a serving platter. Garnish with the liquid from the pan and more fresh rosemary. Finally, add another pinch of salt and serve.

TURKEY CANZANESE

TACCHINO ALLA CANZANESE

INGREDIENTS:

- 15-20 pound fresh turkey
- ½ cup fresh rosemary
- 3 garlic cloves, chopped
- 4 bay leaves, whole
- ¼ cup olive oil
- Salt and fresh black pepper to taste
- Cheesecloth for straining
- Cooking twine

DIRECTIONS:

Bring a full stockpot of water to a boil.

Rinse the turkey under cold water both inside and out. Cut the turkey into two halves and remove the breastbones. Cut off the legs and wings. Place the turkey in a separate large stockpot. Place the rosemary, garlic, and bay leaves inside the turkey and tie the turkey breasts together with twine. Preheat the oven to 350 degrees F.

Place the turkey in a roasting pan with a lid. Pour enough boiling water over the turkey to cover ¾ of the turkey. Add the garlic, spices, bones, wings, and legs to the pot. Place the pot into the oven for 3 hours, turning the turkey occasionally. Remove the turkey breast from the oven after the first 40 minutes. Check to make sure it is cooked through by inserting a knife to check the color. Remove the thread and slice. Arrange the slices on a deep dish platter.

Once the remaining cooking time has finished, filter the broth through the cheesecloth, removing the fat, and ladle over the sliced breast in a deep serving or casserole dish. Line the turkey slices over the broth and place in the refrigerator. Once the gelatin has settled, your turkey is ready to serve.

"This dish comes to us from a neighboring village, Canzano, also in the province of Teramo. Like the Scrippelle Mbusse soup, it was discovered by mistake when cooks realized that turkey broth, prepared in the morning and left to sit became jelly by the evening and that it developed an enhanced flavor. Since this discovery, turkey has been served cold in a bed of jelly. They have even dedicated a holiday "Tacchinando" celebrated from the 24th to the 26th of July in honor of the dish. It became world famous when it was included in the provisions of the first expedition to the moon, led by Neil Armstrong, because of its nutrition, taste, and shelf life." - Elisa

TURKEY
CANZANESE

TACCHINO
ALLA CANZANESE

CHICKEN OR VEAL PARMIGIANO

SERVES 6 PEOPLE

INGREDIENTS:

- Prepared Tomato Marinara Sauce, see my recipe in Sauces, pg.126
- Prepared chicken or veal cutlets see Cutlets recipe, pg. 161, but do not bake them
- 1 pound fresh mozzarella cheese, shredded
- Salt and fresh black pepper to taste
- ½ cup fresh parsley, chopped, including the stem
- ½ cup fresh Pecorino Romano or Parmesan cheese, grated
- 1 portion fresh egg spaghetti or linguine or 1 pound of dry pasta

DIRECTIONS:

Prepare both my Tomato Marinara Sauce and Cutlets Recipes. Prepare and bring a large stockpot of water with a pinch of salt to a boil for the pasta to cook.

Preheat oven to 400 degrees F.

Once you have fried the cutlets, arrange them in a glass casserole dish. Ladle the tomato sauce over the cutlets leaving the tops uncovered. Sprinkle the tops of the cutlets with the mozzarella, Pecorino or Parmesan cheese, and parsley. Bake the cutlets 15 minutes or until the cheese is bubbly. While the cutlets are in the oven, drop your pasta in the boiling water. Cook 3-4 minutes for fresh egg pasta, or follow the instructions on the carton of the dry pasta. Drain your pasta and transfer to a serving bowl and ladle with sauce and grated cheese.

Remove the cutlets from the oven and arrange on a serving platter. Ladle some additional sauce over the cutlets and garnish with grated cheese and fresh parsley. Serve with the pasta.

CUTLETS
COTOLETTE

SERVES 6 PEOPLE

INGREDIENTS:

- 1 pound chicken breasts, veal top round steaks, or lamb chops
- 3 eggs
- 2 cups Italian-style breadcrumbs
- 2 cups vegetable oil
- Salt to taste
- Lemon wedges for garnish

DIRECTIONS:

Rinse the meat of your choice under cold water and drain well. If you are preparing chicken, lay the chicken out on a glass cutting board. Hold your knife parallel to the cutting board and slice the chicken breasts in half so one breast is now two cutlets. Using a meat mallet pound the chicken to create even thickness. If you are using veal or lamb chops, there is no need to slice the meat, but lamb chops will need to be pounded thoroughly to thin out the chop. Be careful not to break the meat away from the bone.

In a glass mixing bowl, beat the eggs. Place the breadcrumbs in a separate bowl. Dip the meat cutlet in the eggs and then into the breadcrumbs, coating evenly on both sides. Place finished cutlets on a plate and refrigerate for 1 hour.

Preheat oven to 350 degrees F. Heat the oil in a large skillet over medium heat. Remove the cutlets from the refrigerator and drop 2-3 cutlets at a time into the oil. Sprinkle with salt while frying. Fry the cutlets for 3-4 minutes on both sides until brown. Remove and pat with a paper towel to remove excess oil. Line the cutlets on a baking sheet and place in the oven. Bake for 20-25 minutes.

ROASTED CHICKEN

POLLO SPEZZATO AL FORNO

SERVES 6-8 PEOPLE

INGREDIENTS:

- 12-14 pieces of chicken legs, thighs, and wings
- 2 garlic cloves, finely chopped
- ¼ cup fresh rosemary
- ¼ cup olive oil
- 1 cup dry white wine
- 2 tablespoons salt
- 1 teaspoon fresh black pepper

DIRECTIONS:

Rinse the chicken pieces under running cold water and pat dry with paper towels. In a large glass mixing bowl, add the garlic, olive oil, wine, pepper, and salt, and beat with a fork to mix thoroughly. Add the chicken pieces to the bowl and cover the chicken pieces with the mixture using your hands. Place the bowl in the refrigerator for 20-30 minutes.

Preheat oven to 375 degrees F.

In a large roasting pan, arrange the chicken pieces, leaving some room between them. Pour the remaining mixture into the pan and garnish with the remaining salt and rosemary.

Place the pan in the oven and roast the legs for 45-60 minutes, checking the pan after 20 minutes. If the pan seems dry, add some water and an additional splash of wine. Test the meat by piercing it with a sharp knife; the juices should be clear and when you cut into the meat, it should fall off the bone. Remove from the oven and arrange on a serving platter and serve.

ROASTED LAMB

AGNELLO SPEZZATO AL FORNO

SERVES 6-8 PEOPLE

INGREDIENTS

- 3 pounds fresh lamb pieces on the bone, or a crown roast
- 6 Idaho potatoes
- 2 garlic cloves, finely chopped
- ¼ cup fresh rosemary
- ¾ cup olive oil
- 1 cup dry white wine
- 2 tablespoons salt
- 1 teaspoon fresh black pepper

DIRECTIONS

Rinse the lamb pieces under cold water and pat dry with paper towels. In a large glass mixing bowl, add the garlic, ¼ cup olive oil, wine, 1 tablespoon salt and pepper and beat with a fork to mix thoroughly. Add the lamb pieces or drop the crown roast chops into the bowl. Place the bowl in the refrigerator for 20-30 minutes.

Peel the potatoes and rinse under cold water. Trim the ends off the potatoes and slice like an apple into 6 even slices. Place the potatoes in a glass mixing bowl and add the remaining olive oil and salt. Mix thoroughly with your hands and set aside.

Preheat oven to 375 degrees F.

In a large roasting pan, arrange the lamb pieces or crown roast in the center of the pan. Arrange the potatoes around the meat and pour the remaining juices from the potatoes and meat over the lamb. Season with an additional pinch of salt and the rosemary.

Place the pan in the oven and roast the lamb for 45-60 minutes, checking the pan after 20 minutes. If the pan seems dry, add some water and an additional splash of wine. Test the meat by piercing it with a sharp knife: the juices should be clear. Remove from the oven and arrange on a platter and serve.

FILLET MIGNON

FILETTO MIGNON

SERVES 6-8 PEOPLE

INGREDIENTS:

- 2-3 pounds whole piece filet mignon
- 1 tablespoon olive oil
- 4 garlic cloves, chopped
- 1 cup dry white wine
- Salt and fresh black pepper to taste

DIRECTIONS:

Rinse the filet under running cold water and pat dry with paper towels. Trim the excess fat. In a large glass mixing bowl, add the garlic, olive oil, and wine, and beat with a fork to mix thoroughly. Add the filet to the bowl. Place the bowl in the refrigerator for 20-30 minutes.

Preheat oven 350 degrees F.

Remove the filet from the refrigerator and place in the center of a roasting pan with a grid. Pour the marinade over the meat and season with salt and pepper. Place in the oven and bake for 35-40 minutes. Turn broiler on and broil for an additional 10 minutes, 5 minutes on each side.

Remove from the oven and slice to desired thickness, then arrange on a serving platter. Pour the juices from the roasting pan over the fillet and serve.

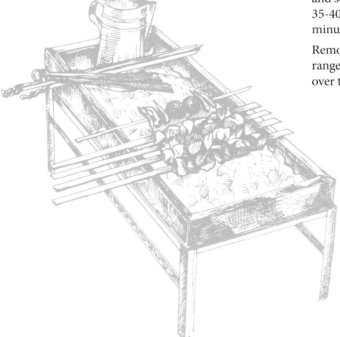

SEAFOOD

SHRIMP WITH CABBAGE AND PANCETTA

SEE PAGE 172

CATCH OF THE DAY

Italian cooking is very regional. That is to say, there is not really one set of Italian recipes that defines the culinary tradition; rather, there are many different interpretations of Italian cooking, with each region of the country drawing influences from its geography.

There are, of course, some core recipes which are similar among the 20 regions of Italy, and there are other dishes that are common to the various parts of Italy, but which are interpreted differently in say, Abruzzi compared with Tuscany or Piedmont. Of course, because every family tends to have its own way of doing things, no two households would ever prepare the same dish in the same manner even if they were situated next door to one another, and so each family tends to redefine what one thinks of Italian food.

By and large, each of Italy's regions has its own culinary tradition. The diverse geography of this relatively small nation—from the mountainous north to the coastal towns to the islands—has given rise to several distinct culinary traditions. In addition, it was not really until the post–World War II era that a legitimate system of highways was finally built connecting the disparate geographic locales. Previous to this, it was not all that common for people to leave the region they grew up in, and in most cases, to leave the town or village in which they were born. Today, it is still traditional in many parts of the country for an entire family to live within 10 miles of one another. It would be wonderful to think that sons and daughters of Italian families stay in close proximity to their parents out of love and affection.

In many cases this is true, yet the historical lack of highways and byways probably had an influence as well: people did not move away because they could not travel very far all that effectively. And if people did not move around much, neither did their recipes.

I believe that this sense of isolation has influenced my own experience and in my style of cooking. Where we lived, in Poggio Valle, being disconnected from conveniences produced a sense of self-reliance. Because we could not run to the grocery store when we needed supplies, we had to be very careful to use every part of our ingredients and we had to be diligent about saving some for later. I have already described these influences when discussing how we would smoke and dry meat so that we could maintain a supply without the aid of refrigeration.

Like many Italians, where I grew up influenced what kinds of ingredients we had access to, and therefore, dictated what we considered the main staples of our diet. In our village, we saw the fish monger only on occasion—and during the winter months, when the local roads were nearly impassable, we would not see fresh fish in our town for months at a time. And by the time the fish monger finally reached our little village after having visited a few others before ours, what he or she had available for sale was extremely limited.

Given these conditions it is not hard to see why so many of the dishes we prepared in our village (and that are included in this book) are based around meats and vegetables: meats because we could raise and then butcher livestock, and fruits and vegetables because we were children of the land. When we did have access to seafood, it was usually salted and preserved. On occasion, we were fortunate to get shrimp or other shellfish; these were usually served in celebratory meals rather than being everyday ingredients in our food.

Many are familiar with the tradition of the seven fishes and think that this is a traditional Italian meal served during the holiday season. I would suggest, however, that this is more an Italian-American custom; in fact, I do not know of many Italian families that follow this tradition to this day. I would guess that a great number of the seafood dishes regularly celebrated as traditional Italian either hail from regions of Italy closer to the sea, or else materialized among pockets of Italian-American immigrants.

In the following chapter, I will focus on seafood dishes. There are a few that are based on older recipes with which I arrived in America, but mostly what is presented on these pages are recipes I learned through experimentation after I arrived in my new homeland. That is to say, I conceived many of these dishes only because it became easier to buy seafood ingredients at my local market rather than having to wait for the fish monger to arrive in our small village.

STUFFED MUSSELS

COZZE RIPIENE AL FORNO

SERVES 4-6 PEOPLE

INGREDIENTS:

- 2 pounds fresh mussels
- 3½ cups stale Italian bread, grated but coarse
- ½ cup fresh parsley, chopped, including the stem
- ¼ cup fresh oregano, chopped
- 1 garlic clove, pressed
- 1 teaspoon salt
- 1 teaspoon fresh black pepper
- 2 eggs
- 1 cup Pecorino Romano Cheese, grated
- 1½ cup olive oil

DIRECTIONS:

Preheat oven to 400 degrees F.

Scrub the mussels under cold water and place the cleaned mussels in a medium- sized saucepan. Add 1½ cups water and place on high heat. Allow the mussels to open and remove immediately from the saucepan with a ladle and place in a bowl. Do not discard the water from the saucepan. Remove the part of the shell that is not attached to the mussel, and arrange the shells with the mussels in a roasting pan.

In a separate mixing bowl, add the grated bread, parsley, oregano, garlic, salt and pepper and mix with a spoon. Beat in the eggs and blend thoroughly. Add the cheese and any liquid left from the bowl of mussels and saucepan and blend through.

Spoon the mixture over the mussels, one by one and cover the entire shell. Drizzle the olive oil over the mussels and bake in the oven for 8-10 minutes until lightly crispy on top.

Remove and arrange on a serving platter; garnish with parsley.

"This is a recipe shared with me by my sister-in-law Franca. Her specialty is preparing seafood dishes, and she often hosts friends and family for a 24-course seafood dinner." - Elisa

AROMATIC SALMON
SALMONE AROMATICO

SERVES 6 PEOPLE

INGREDIENTS:

- 6 salmon steaks (6-8 ounces each)
- ½ cup fennel, chopped
- 1 garlic clove, pressed
- ½ cup fresh parsley, chopped, including the stem
- 1 cup Italian breadcrumbs
- ½ teaspoon cumin seeds
- 1 tablespoon paprika
- 1 teaspoon fresh black pepper
- 1 teaspoon salt
- 2 lemons
- 1 cup olive oil

DIRECTIONS:

Preheat oven to 450 degrees F.

Grate 1 whole lemon. In a food processor, combine the fennel, garlic, parsley, breadcrumbs, cumin, paprika, pepper, salt, and lemon zest. Crush or process until coarse. Pour ½ cup of olive oil into a bowl large enough to dip one piece of the salmon. Pour the breadcrumb mixture into a separate bowl of equal size. Drop a piece of salmon into the oil and turn over, then drop into the breadcrumb mixture skin side up. Remove and place the uncoated side down onto a plate.

Heat the other ½ cup of olive oil in a sauté pan over medium-high heat. Add the salmon, 2-3 pieces at a time, breadcrumb side up and cook for 3 minutes. Transfer the salmon to a roasting pan and bake in the oven for 10 minutes. While the salmon is baking, slice the remaining lemon in wedges. Remove the salmon from the oven and arrange on a serving plate. Garnish with the lemon wedges and serve.

MY SEVEN FISHES STEW

CIOPPINO

SERVES 8-10 PEOPLE

INGREDIENTS:

- 1 pound small clams or mussels
- 1 pound medium-sized shrimp, shelled and deveined
- 1 pound fresh squid with tentacles, rinsed and chopped into ½ -inch thick rings
- 2 pounds large bay scallops, sliced in halves
- 1 pound tilapia, cut into 1-inch cubes
- 1 pound flounder, cut into 1-inch cubes
- 1 cup olive oil
- 4 garlic cloves, chopped
- ½ cup parsley, chopped, including the stem
- 1 bay leaf
- 4 pounds fresh tomatoes, peeled and chopped, or 3 28-ounce cans of crushed tomatoes
- 1 cup water
- Salt and fresh black pepper to taste
- ¼ cup fresh Pecorino Romano or Parmesan cheese, grated
- 2 portions fresh egg Tagliatelle, see my recipe in Pastas, pg. 52 or 2 pounds of box pasta, optional

DIRECTIONS:

Scrub the clams or mussels under cold water and place in water-filled bowl with 2 tablespoons salt, and soak for 30 minutes; rinse thoroughly and drain. Set aside. Heat 1 cup of the olive oil in a large saucepan over medium heat. Add the garlic, parsley, and squid and sauté for 5 minutes.

Add the tomatoes, bay leaf, and water and simmer for 30 minutes. Reduce the heat to low and add the shrimp, scallops, tilapia, and flounder; allow to simmer for an additional 30 minutes. While the fish is cooking, bring a large stockpot of water with a pinch of salt to a boil for the pasta. Add the clams or mussels to the sauce. Add a pinch or two of salt and pepper to your liking.

When the water begins to boil, drop pasta in and cook accordingly: 3-5 minutes for fresh pasta, or follow the instructions on box. Drain pasta and place in a large serving bowl.

Remove ½ the stew and place in a separate serving bowl for the table. Ladle the remaining stew over the pasta. Remove any unopened shells. Garnish with some cheese and serve.

MY SEVEN FISHES STEW
CIOPPINO

SHRIMP WITH CABBAGE AND PANCETTA

GAMBERI CON CAPPUCCIO E PANCETTA

SERVES 6 PEOPLE

INGREDIENTS:

- 4 pounds large shrimp, shelled and deveined
- 1 pound pancetta or bacon, cut into 1-inch cubes
- 4 cups green cabbage, shredded
- 14-16 scallions, chopped, including the stems
- 5 garlic cloves, chopped
- 1 long hot red pepper, diced
- 2 teaspoons salt
- 1 teaspoon fresh black pepper
- 2 cups fresh basil leaves, whole
- 3 tablespoons olive oil

DIRECTIONS:

Bring a large pot of salted water to boil. Add the cabbage and boil for 20-25 minutes, cooking until tender.

Heat the olive oil in a large, deep skillet with a lid over a high flame. Add the pancetta and sauté for 3-5 minutes, until lightly browned. Add the cabbage and cook another 5 minutes, covered; remove lid after 2 minutes and give the cabbage a good stir, then cover for remaining 2 minutes. Stir in the scallions and shrimp, and sauté until the scallions soften and the shrimp turns pink. Add the garlic, salt, black and red pepper and continue to sauté uncovered for an additional 3-4 minutes so the shrimp can cook through completely.

Transfer to a serving bowl, fold in the basil leaves, and serve.

MUSSELS IN RED SAUCE

COZZE FRA DIAVOLO

INGREDIENTS:

FOR THE MUSSELS:

- 4 pounds fresh mussels
- 2 tablespoons olive oil
- 5 garlic cloves, peeled and chopped
- 1 cup white wine
- 3 cups tomato sauce
- ¼ cup of fresh parsley, chopped, including the stem
- 2 tablespoons red pepper flakes

FOR THE SAUCE:

- 4 35-ounce cans crushed tomatoes
- ½ cup olive oil
- 4 bay leaves
- 1 full head garlic, chopped
- 3 large white onions, sliced in halves
- 2 carrots, cut into thirds
- 2 celery stalks, cut into thirds
- 1 8-ounce can tomato paste
- ¼ cup fresh oregano, chopped
- ¼ cup fresh parsley, chopped
- 3 teaspoons salt
- 2 tablespoons red pepper flakes
- 1 teaspoon fresh black pepper
- 1-1 ½ pounds dry spaghetti

DIRECTIONS:

In a large saucepan, prepare the sauce. Add the olive oil and garlic to the saucepan and sauté over medium heat for 5 minutes until garlic begins to brown. Add the onions, carrots, and celery and continue to sauté for 5 minutes. Stir occasionally to prevent them from scorching.

Add the crushed tomatoes, the tomato paste, bay leaves, parsley, oregano, salt, pepper, and 2 cups of water; allow to come to a boil. Lower the heat and simmer, partially covered for at least one hour. For best results I allow it to simmer for two hours and add an additional cup of water. Stir occasionally to prevent sticking.

Before you are ready to add the pasta, spoon out the vegetables and onions and set aside. Prepare a separate stockpot with water to boil the pasta. As pasta water begins to boil, it is time to prepare the mussels. In a large sauté pan, heat the olive oil over medium heat. Add the garlic and red pepper, and sauté for 2 minutes. Add the white wine and the tomato sauce from the saucepan, cover, and bring to a boil.

Add the mussels and replace the lid. Cook over high heat for 3 minutes. Remove the lid, stir and continue to cook until the mussels are completely open. Remove from heat.

Drain pasta and place in a large serving bowl. Spoon the mussels over the pasta, and add enough tomato sauce to cover the pasta. Toss gently and add more sauce. Garnish with the bay leaves from the sauce, red pepper flakes, and some shredded Pecorino Romano cheese.

SHRIMP & ARTICHOKE RISOTTO

RISOTTO DI GAMBERI E CARCIOFI

INGREDIENTS:

- 10 baby artichokes
- 1 lemon zest
- 2 tablespoons olive oil
- 1 shallot, finely chopped
- ½ cup dry white wine
- 1½ cups Arborio rice
- 8-10 cups seafood or vegetable stock
- 2 pounds small shrimp, peeled and cleaned
- Salt and freshly ground black pepper to taste

DIRECTIONS:

Using a knife cut off the prickly top third of the baby artichokes and discard. Pull back each dark outer leaf and snap it off. Use a vegetable peeler or paring knife to remove the tough outer layers. Slice the cleaned artichokes into pieces about ½ -inch thick. Place them in a bowl of water with some lemon juice. Place the stock into a large saucepan, and bring it to a simmer over low heat. Heat the oil in a skillet over medium heat. Add the chopped shallot and a pinch of salt, and sauté until tender. Drain the artichokes, add them to skillet, and stir for five minutes until they begin to soften.

Add the rice and stir until the grains are well coated and begin to crackle. Add the wine and stir over medium heat until the rice has absorbed it. Add two ladles of the simmering stock, enough to cover the rice. Cook, stirring often, until the liquid is almost absorbed. Add another ladleful or two of the stock, and continue to cook, adding more stock when the rice is almost dry. It will take 20-25 minutes to completely prepare the rice. Add the shrimp and lemon zest along with another ladleful of stock. Stir to combine for about 30 seconds and turn off the heat. Continue to stir so that the residual heat finishes cooking the shrimp, until they just turn pink. If it appears too dry, add another ladleful of stock to loosen it. Season with salt and pepper and finish with a drizzle of olive oil. Serve immediately.

WHITE WINE SHELLFISH STEW
FRUTTI DI MARE CON VINO BIANCO

INGREDIENTS:

- 2 pounds fresh clams
- 2 pounds fresh mussels
- 2 pounds fresh oysters
- 2 garlic cloves, chopped
- 1½ cups dry white wine
- ¼ cup olive oil
- ¼ cup fresh parsley, chopped, including the stem
- 2 pounds fresh tomatoes, peeled and chopped
- Salt and fresh black pepper to taste

DIRECTIONS:

Scrub all the shells under cold running water. In a large sauté pan, add the olive oil, parsley, and garlic and sauté over medium heat until the garlic is golden brown. Add the clams, mussels, oysters, tomatoes, and wine. Add a pinch of salt and pepper, and cook for 15 minutes, or until most of the shells have opened. Discard any shells that do not open.

Transfer to a serving bowl and serve with fresh Italian bread to soak up the juices.

SPICY SHRIMP SCAMPI
SCAMPI PICCANTE

INGREDIENTS:

- 2 pounds small fresh shrimp, peeled and deveined
- 4 tablespoons butter or margarine
- ½ cup olive oil
- 1 teaspoon salt
- ¼ cup of fresh parsley, chopped, including the stems
- 1 teaspoon dried red peppers, crushed
- 2 garlic cloves, crushed
- 1½ pound dry angel hair pasta

DIRECTIONS:

Bring a large stockpot of water with a pinch of salt to a boil. In a large skillet over medium heat, melt the butter. Add the oil olive and garlic and sauté for 2-3 minutes. Add the shrimp, parsley, salt, and red pepper. Sauté the shrimp for 3-4 minutes while stirring frequently.

Remove from heat. Cook pasta according to the package instructions, drain and transfer to a serving bowl. Add shrimp and sauce and toss. Serve immediately.

OPTIONAL:
YOU CAN ALSO ADD A ¼ CUP OF DRY WHITE WINE BEFORE YOU SAUTÉ THE SHRIMP.

BROILED BACCALA

BACCALÀ ALLA GRIGLIA

SERVES 4-6 PEOPLE

INGREDIENTS:

- 1 pound dried salt cod
- ½ cup olive oil
- 3 garlic cloves, chopped
- ¼ cup parsley, chopped, including the stem
- Salt and fresh black pepper to taste

DIRECTIONS:

Cut the cod into 3-inch strips and place in a glass bowl full of cold water. Refrigerate for 2 days, changing the water daily. Drain the strips and place in a bowl with the olive oil, garlic, and parsley. Transfer to a roasting pan and garnish the top with a pinch of salt and pepper. Broil for 10-15 minutes. The Baccala should brown nicely. Remove from the oven and arrange on a serving platter and serve.

FRIED SMELTS

SPERLANI FRITTI

" On Christmas Eve, I prepare both sizes of these crispy treats. The children prefer the mini smelts and call them French fries." - Elisa

INGREDIENTS:

- 2 pounds large fresh smelts, cleaned, gutted and heads removed; or 4 pounds of mini smelts, cleaned and heads removed
- 3-4 cups all-purpose flour
- 3-4 cups vegetable oil, for frying
- Salt to taste

DIRECTIONS:

Rinse the smelts and place in a colander to drain excess water. Season with salt. Place the flour in a large bowl and drop in 2-3 smelts at a time to cover evenly with a thick layer of flour. Remove and shake off any loose flour. Heat the oil in a large, deep sauté pan. The level of oil should be high enough to submerge the smelts. When the oil is hot, drop the smelts in one-by-one, taking care not to overcrowd the pan. Fry the smelts for about 5-10 minutes or until the desired level of crispness is achieved. Remove the smelts and allow them to drain on a paper towel-covered wire rack. Transfer to a serving platter and serve.

FRIED SMELTS

SPERLANI FRITTI

FRIED CALAMARI

CALAMARI FRITTI

INGREDIENTS:

- 1 pound fresh squid with tentacles, rinsed and cut into ½-inch thick rings
- 2 cups all-purpose flour
- 1 pinch red pepper, ground
- 2 cups vegetable oil
- ¼ cup fresh parsley, finely chopped
- 1 pinch salt
- 1 pinch fresh black pepper
- Lemons and or marinara sauce for dipping

DIRECTIONS:

Rinse the squid and place in a colander to drain excess water. Place the flour in a large bowl. Blend in the parsley, salt, and red and black pepper. Drop in several rings at a time and cover evenly with a thick layer of flour. Remove and shake off any extra flour. Heat the oil in a large, deep sauté pan. The level of oil should be high enough to submerge the rings. When the oil is hot, drop the rings in one-by-one, taking care not to overcrowd the pan. Fry the rings for 1 minute, just enough for them to form a golden color. Remove the rings with tongs and allow them to drain on a paper towel-covered wire rack. Transfer to a serving platter and serve with lemon wedges or a side of marinara sauce.

SAUTÉED BACCALA

INGREDIENTS:

- 1 pound dried salt cod
- ½ cup olive oil
- 3 garlic cloves, chopped
- ¼ cup parsley, chopped, including the stem
- 2 pounds fresh tomatoes, peeled and chopped or 1 28-ounce can of crushed tomatoes
- Salt and fresh black pepper to taste

DIRECTIONS:

Cut the cod into 3-inch strips, and place in a glass bowl full of cold water. Refrigerate for 2 days, changing the water daily. Drain the strips and place in a bowl with the olive oil. Place a large sauté pan over medium heat, and add the Baccala and garlic. Sauté for 2-3 minutes.

Reduce the heat and add the tomatoes and parsley. Simmer for 1 hour. Remove from heat and place in a serving bowl.

FRIED CALAMARI
CALAMARI FRITTI

CLAMS CASINO

VONGOLE AL FORNO

SERVES 6 PEOPLE

INGREDIENTS:

- 2 pounds large fresh clams, scrubbed
- 1 tablespoon plus 2 tablespoons olive oil
- ½ cup pancetta, finely chopped
- 1 cup red bell pepper, finely chopped
- ½ cup shallots, finely chopped
- 2 garlic cloves, minced
- ½ cup Italian-style breadcrumbs
- ½ cup dry white wine, plus some for cooking.
- Fresh Pecorino Romano or Parmesan cheese, grated
- Salt and fresh black pepper to taste
- 2 lemons, sliced into wedges

DIRECTIONS:

Preheat oven to 400 degrees F.

Place the clams with 2 cups of water and 1 tablespoon of olive oil in a large sauté pan over medium heat. Allow the clams to simmer until they open. Remove the opened clams from the pan and break off the top shell. In a large glass bowl, add the pancetta, bell pepper, shallots, garlic, olive oil, and wine and mix thoroughly with your hands. Add the breadcrumbs and mix thoroughly. Arrange the clams in a casserole dish or two. Spoon 1 to 1½ tablespoons of the mixture over each clam and press down. Season the top of the clams with some salt and pepper. Pour a shot glass worth of wine into a bowl and use a brush to gently wipe the tops of the clams with the wine. Pour the remaining wine into the bottom of the casserole dish.

Spread the grated cheese over the tops and place in the oven. Bake until the clam tops turn a golden brown color, roughly 10-15 minutes. Remove from the oven and arrange on a serving platter. Garnish with lemon wedges.

MY MENTOR – ZIA IDA

I have mentioned in other parts of this book that I owe a great deal of gratitude to my Zia Ida. She was my first cooking mentor and she truly taught me so much about food and about life. But I have perhaps undersold how much she was celebrated and sought after as a chef in our little village of Poggio Valle.

In fact, Zia Ida was in great demand to cook for just about every special occasion I can recall. It was also not unusual for families in neighboring villages to make a request for her to come and prepare her special meals for their fetes and festivities. She took great pride in this fact, and if you ask me, the accolades were well deserved.

When I married, it seemed obvious that my aunt should cook for our event. But, as you may imagine, cooking for an event like that is a total commitment. If Zia Ida had spent the day in the kitchen, she would have missed the ceremony and the gathering of family. My father realized this and intended to ban Zia Ida from the kitchen that day; the only way to do this, of course, was to invite her as a guest. If we had not, Ida would have spent the whole day in the kitchen anyway fussing over the meal and preparation. I wonder if she might even have caused some unrest, barking commands at servants not technically under her charge.

Ultimately, I had a wonderful wedding day, even if my aunt did not prepare our meal. It certainly would have been memorable if she had; at the same time, I am also thankful that I got to spend that day with her outside the kitchen celebrating our joyous occasion.

Fortunately, I had many other occasions to cook alongside Zia Ida, but one time in particular stands out in my mind when I traveled back to Italy to celebrate my parents' 50th wedding anniversary. Such an occasion called for a special festivity, and we intended to pull out all the stops to prepare a very special meal.

Our humble little village had not changed much since I had left. There were still no major markets in Poggio Valle, so we knew we would have to go to the nearby city to pick up supplies, just as I had done so many times years before as a child. Fortunately, the roads had been vastly improved by then so that the travel itself would not be hard—although, it might be more appropriate to say that I was happy there was any road at all, as the road I remembered passing along in my youth was barely navigable even in the best of conditions.

It was a sticky July day when we set off to the market to get ingredients and supplies for the party, and the heat was nearly unbearable. We had a lot of preparation to do and not a lot of time to spend worrying about the weather. For one thing, we had decided to get some live chickens from the market, which would be the easy part. As you can imagine, it would take time and a lot of effort to get them ready for cooking—butchering, plucking feathers, and the like.

After we had secured our poultry requirement, we still had much shopping to do, and so, sweet Zia Ida put the chickens—the live chickens, mind you—in the trunk of the car so that we could continue to shop.

A few hours later, we returned to the car, the sun and the heat baking us, sweat pouring from our brows; but that heat was also starting to cook our feathered friends. When we opened the trunk of the car, the poor chickens were a pitiful site, very lethargic and nearly lifeless. We feared that the unplanned chicken roast would ruin an important part of our menu, but none of us quite knew what to do. None of us, that is, except for Zia Ida, our family chef and a woman known for her inherent practicality.

Imagine this scene if you will: there we stood, right in the middle of the Piazza Garibaldi - near lifeless chickens in the trunk of the car. If they died before we were ready for them, they could spoil and potentially ruin our meal. And so, that is how it came to be that, right in the middle of the piazza, Zia Ida seized each of the birds in her hands and twisted their necks.

I can only imagine the spectacle of this whole scene and what it must have looked like to anyone who ventured to look our way. I still laugh about this day, and it fills me with such joy to think of this story that so perfectly represents who my Zia Ida was, a woman who would let nothing alter her agenda in the kitchen.

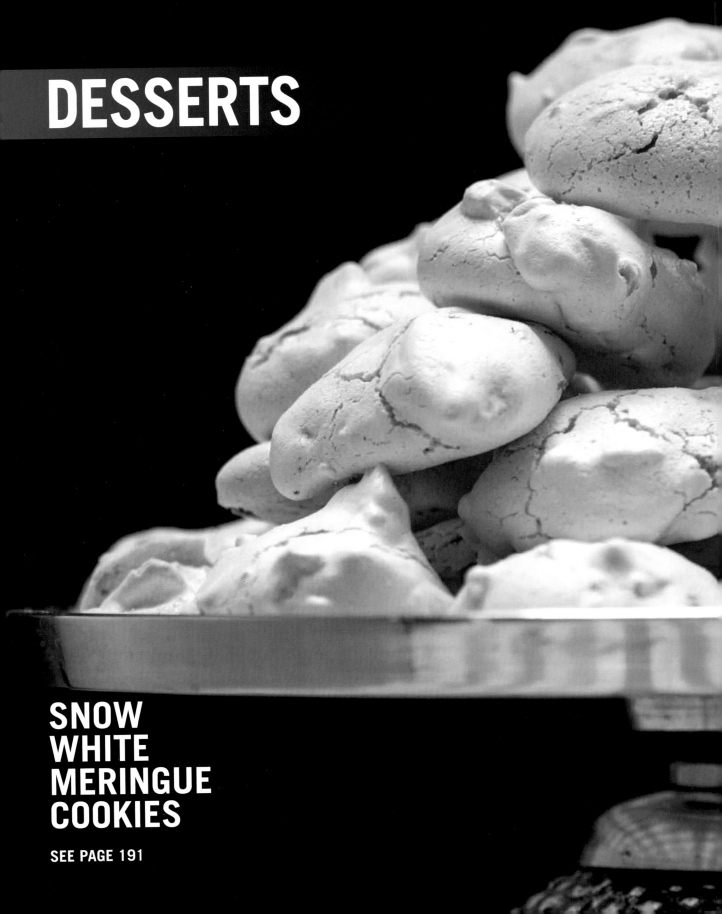

DESSERTS

SNOW WHITE MERINGUE COOKIES

SEE PAGE 191

AMARETTI COOKIES

AMARETTI

MAKES APPROX. 4 DOZEN COOKIES

INGREDIENTS

- 3 large eggs, separated
- 1¼ cups plus 1 tablespoon sugar
- 4 cups almond meal flour
- 1 teaspoon lemon juice
- 1 cup confectioners' sugar, for rolling Silver or pearl ball cake decorations, for decorating

DIRECTIONS

With an electric mixer, whisk the egg yolks. Gradually add sugar, whisking until well combined. Add the almond flour; whisk at low speed, do not over mix. In a separate bowl, beat the egg whites on high speed to a soft peak. Using a large spatula, fold one-third of the egg whites into the almond mixture and blend with the spatula. Add the lemon juice and the remaining egg whites and blend until dough forms. Cover and refrigerate amaretti cookie batter for at least one hour, or overnight if you have the time.

Preheat oven to 325 degrees F. Roll amaretti dough into balls the size of small walnuts, coat in confectioners' sugar and place a candy decoration in the top center. Roll 20 amaretti cookies for each parchment paper-covered baking sheet. Bake until lightly golden, about 25 to 30 minutes. Remove and cool cookies on a wire rack.

APPLE CAKE
TORTA DI MELE

SERVES 12-15 PEOPLE

INGREDIENTS:

- 4 eggs
- 3 cups all-purpose flour
- 2 cups sugar
- 1 cup vegetable oil
- 3 teaspoons baking powder
- 3 teaspoons vanilla extract
- ½ cup orange juice
- 4 cups Red Delicious apples
- 2 tablespoons cinnamon
- An additional 3 tablespoons of sugar

DIRECTIONS:

Preheat oven to 350 degrees F.

Prepare the apples. Peel and slice the apples and place in a mixing bowl. Add the cinnamon and the 3 tablespoons of sugar and mix together. Set aside. In an electric mixing bowl, slowly add the eggs and sugar and beat for 5 minutes; add the flour, baking powder, oil, and orange juice and mix until all ingredients are blended well.

Using a ring or Bundt pan with a hole, grease the bottom and sides of the pan, and pour 2 inches of batter into the pan. Then arrange the apple slices evenly around the pan on top of the batter. Next add another 2 inches of batter and repeat the layer of apple slices. Pour the remaining batter into the pan and dress the top with the remaining slices in a circular design.

Bake 1½ hours until lightly brown, and insert a toothpick in the center. If nothing sticks to the toothpick, the cake is ready. Remove immediately from the pan, freeing the edges with a knife and let cool.

LEMON SPONGE CAKE
PANE DI SPAGNA

SERVES 10 TO 12 PEOPLE

INGREDIENTS:

- 8 eggs
- 2 cups sugar
- 2½ cups all-purpose flour
- 3 teaspoons lemon juice
- 3 teaspoons baking powder
- 1 cup vegetable oil
- ½ cup water

"This is a cake that I bake regularly, to have in case a friend or neighbor pays me an unexpected visit for a cup of coffee. My grandson Sebastian likes to have this cake for breakfast, by soaking a piece in a mug of warm milk or hot tea. He calls it Breakfast Porridge." - Elisa

DIRECTIONS:

Preheat oven to 350 degrees F.

With an electric mixer, beat the eggs and sugar until creamy at high speed. Reduce the speed to a medium-low, sift in the flour gradually, and add the baking powder. Mix for 3 minutes, then add the lemon juice, vegetable oil, and water. Continue to mix until batter is smooth and well blended.

Using a ring or Bundt pan with a hole, grease the bottom and sides of the pan, and pour the batter into the pan.

Bake for 45 minutes, until the top is lightly brown. Test the center of the cake with a toothpick and make sure it does not stick. Remove from the oven and let cool for 5 minutes. Using a knife, loosen the edges and turn the cake over onto a wire rack. Gently turn the cake upright and cool on a wire rack.

CHOCOLATE COOKIES

DOLCI AL CIOCCOLATOO

MAKES APPROX. 9 DOZEN COOKIES

INGREDIENTS:

- 5 eggs
- 1½ teaspoons ground cloves
- 2 cups sugar
- 7 cups all-purpose flour
- 1½ teaspoons allspice
- 1 teaspoon salt
- 1 cup unsweetened cocoa powder
- ¼ cup baking powder
- 1½ teaspoons cinnamon
- Zest of 1 large orange
- ½ cup vegetable shortening
- ½ cup salted butter
- 1 teaspoon vanilla extract
- ¼ cup orange juice
- ¼ cup whole milk or heavy cream
- 8 ounces cream cheese
- ½ cup chopped walnuts (optional)
- ½ cup confectioners' sugar

DIRECTIONS:

Preheat oven to 350 degrees F.

Whisk flour, sugar, cocoa powder, baking powder, cinnamon, cloves, allspice, and salt in a large mixing bowl. Stir orange zest into flour mixture. Add vegetable shortening and butter into the mixture, using your hands, until crumbly.

With an electric mixer, beat eggs and vanilla extract until foamy. Add egg mixture, ¼ cup orange juice, ¼ cup milk to flour mixture and knead dough in the bowl until thoroughly combined and dough doesn't stick to your hands. Dough will be stiff. Knead cream cheese thoroughly into dough, followed by walnuts (optional). Wrap dough in plastic wrap and place in refrigerator for 20 minutes. Form dough into balls about 1½ inches in diameter and place onto ungreased baking sheets.

Bake cookies in the preheated oven until lightly browned, 12 to 14 minutes. Cool cookies on wire racks. Once cool, sift confectioners' sugar on top.

BOURBON BALLS

INGREDIENTS:

- 6 ounces semi-sweet chocolate
- 3 tablespoons light Karo Syrup
- ½ cup bourbon or rum
- 2 ½ cups vanilla wafers, crushed
- ½ cup confectioners' sugar
- 1 cup walnuts, finely chopped

DIRECTIONS:

Crush the wafers in a food processor. Using a double boiler, melt the chocolate, stirring repeatedly to avoid burning. Add the bourbon and Karo syrup.

Add the crushed wafers and nuts to the mixture and blend thoroughly. Set aside for 30 minutes. Shape into balls the size of a small walnut. Roll each ball evenly in the sugar and store in an airtight container and let stand for 2 to 3 days.

BREAKFAST BISCOTTI

"This is an easy and quick biscotti recipe that is perfect for dipping in milk or tea. It is a favorite of all my grandchildren." - Elisa

INGREDIENTS:

- 3 eggs
- ½ cup sugar
- ½ cup of vegetable oil
- 1 teaspoon vanilla extract
- 1½ - 2 cups all-purpose flour, depending on the size of eggs, smaller eggs will require more flour
- 3 teaspoons baking powder
- Rainbow or chocolate jimmies for decorating

DIRECTIONS:

Preheat oven to 350 degrees F.

In an electric mixer beat the eggs. Add the oil, flour, sugar, vanilla extract and baking powder and mix until you have a consistent mixture.

Line a cookie sheet with waxed paper. Using a tablespoon, scoop a tablespoon of the mixture one at a time and place on the baking sheet 2 inches from the edge. The teaspoons of mixture should overlap each other to form a log the length of the cookie sheet. You should be able to form 2 logs on the cookie sheet. Sprinkle the top with your favorite jimmies.

Place in the oven and bake for 20-25 minutes. Remove from the oven and allow to cool. Slice the logs into 1-1½ -inch slices.

IMPOSSIBLE COCONUT CREAM PIE

INGREDIENTS:

- 4 large eggs
- ½ stick margarine
- 1 teaspoon vanilla extract
- 2 cups whole milk
- ¾ cup sugar
- ½ cup Bisquick
- 8 ounces Philadelphia Cream Cheese
- 14-ounce bag coconut flakes

DIRECTIONS:

Preheat oven to 350 degrees F.

First, melt the margarine in a small saucepan. In a blender combine the eggs, melted margarine, and milk and mix. Add the sugar, Bisquick, cream cheese and continue to blend. Finally, gradually add the coconut and blend until the mixture is consistent.

Grease a 12-inch metal pie plate and pour the mixture into the pan. Place a cookie sheet on the shelf beneath the pie pan and place the pie into the oven.

Cook 55 minutes. Remove from oven and cool. Once the pie has cooled to room temperature, place it in the refrigerator until it is time to serve; this pie is best served chilled.

"This pie is called Impossible, because it is hard to believe how easy it is to make. You also do not prepare any crust, so it is great for those calorie-conscious guests. Next door neighbor, Maria Halpin, shared this recipe with me, when she moved next door to me on Westbury Drive in Overbrook, Philadelphia" - Elisa

DOUBLE CHOCOLATE BISCOTTI

BISCOTTI AL DOPPIO CIOCCOLATO

MAKES APPROX. 4-5 DOZEN COOKIES

INGREDIENTS:

- 2 eggs
- 2 cups all-purpose flour
- ¼ cup cocoa powder
- 1½ teaspoons baking powder
- ½ teaspoon salt
- 1 stick salted butter
- 1¼ cups sugar
- 1 teaspoon vanilla extract
- 1 cup almonds, chopped
- ½ cup mini semi-sweet chocolate chips

DIRECTIONS:

Preheat oven to 350 degrees F.

Place almonds evenly spaced on a baking sheet and place in oven. Roasting will take approximately 20 minutes depending on your oven. Occasionally mix the nuts with a wooden spoon for even browning. Remove the roasted almonds from the stove and set aside. Chop the almonds once they have cooled.

With an electric mixer, cream the eggs, butter, and sugar. Add the flour, cocoa powder, baking powder, salt, vanilla extract, chocolate chips, and roasted almonds. Blend until all the ingredients are mixed well and the dough is an even brown color. Flour a clean surface and divide the dough into 5 equal parts. Roll out each piece to approximately 2-inches wide. Place each log onto a waxed paper-covered cookie sheet, and bake for 30 minutes.

Remove from the oven and let cool. I tend not to toast the biscotti, but if you like, once the logs cool, slice into pieces about ½-inch thick, line the biscotti back on the cookie sheet, and toast for 10 minutes. Remove from oven and cool on wire racks.

"Although she has enjoyed and grown to love many of our family dishes, these biscotti top the favorite list of my granddaughter-in-law Julie." - Elisa

HALF MOONS
BISCOTTI MEZZA LUNA

MAKES APPROX. 3 DOZEN COOKIES

INGREDIENTS:

- 2 eggs
- ½ pound salted butter, softened
- 2½ cups all-purpose flour
- ½ cup sugar
- ½ cup confectioners' sugar
- 2 tablespoons orange juice
- 2 teaspoons vanilla extract
- 16 ounces semi-sweet, dark, or white chocolate chips, optional
- 3 teaspoons shortening

DIRECTIONS:

With an electric mixer, cream the butter, sugar, and confectioners' sugar. Add 1 egg, orange juice, and vanilla extract and continue to mix until blended through. Gradually sift the flour into the mixture. Wrap the dough in plastic wrap and place in the refrigerator for 1 hour.

In a small bowl, beat the remaining egg, and set aside for later. Pre-heat oven to 350 degrees F for 15 minutes before removing the dough from the refrigerator.

Using a rolling pin, roll out dough on a lightly floured surface so the dough is ¼ of an inch thick. Cut the dough into 4-inch x 1½-inch rectangles. Curve the ends of the cut outs into a half moon shape and place on waxed paper-covered cookie sheet about 1½ inches apart. Brush the tops of the cookies on the sheet with the beaten egg.

Bake for 12-15 minutes until lightly brown. Remove cookies and place on a wire rack to cool. You can serve the cookies just like this, or add the chocolate for a better presentation. Heat the chocolate and shortening until the mixture is creamy. Remove the mixture from heat and dip the ends of the cookies into the chocolate and place on waxed paper. Top with nuts or sprinkles for added presentation.

ORANGE COOKIES
DOLCI ALL'ARANCIA

MAKES APPROX. 5 TO 6 DOZEN COOKIES

INGREDIENTS:

- 4 medium eggs
- 1 egg yolk
- 5½ cups all-purpose flour
- 2 cups white sugar
- 1 tablespoon of baking powder
- 1 cup Crisco
- ½ cup orange juice
- 1 teaspoon vanilla extract
- 2 drops orange food coloring, substitute with 1 yellow & 1 red
- 1 cup confectioners' sugar

DIRECTIONS:

Preheat oven to 350 degrees F.

In a small saucepan, melt the Crisco, then remove from heat and cool to room temperature. With an electric mixer at slow speed, beat eggs and sugar, then add the flour and baking powder. Once mixed together, add the orange juice, food coloring, Crisco and vanilla extract.

Place the confectioners' sugar in a bowl, drop a tablespoon of the dough into the sugar and roll into a ball; place on a greased, or waxed paper-covered, cookie sheet at least 2 inches apart. Bake for 25-30 minutes until lightly brown. Remove and cool on wire rack.

ALMOND BRITTLE
CROCCANTE

INGREDIENTS:

- 1 tablespoon honey
- 1¼ cups sugar
- 3 cups almonds, skinless, blanched and slivered

DIRECTIONS:

Preheat oven to 300 degrees F.

On a cookie sheet spread the almonds evenly, and place in oven to warm for 5 minutes. Do not allow to brown.

In a medium saucepan, melt the honey and sugar, mixing gently with a spoon until they achieve a golden brown color. Add the almonds to the mixture and continue to stir for 5-10 minutes.

Pour the mixture onto a cold marble or granite surface. If you do not have this, use a glass cutting board. Roll the mixture out to roughly ½-inch thick. Allow settling for a few minutes, then cut into desired shapes and cool on a wire rack.

SNOW WHITE MERINGUE COOKIES

MAKES 2 DOZEN COOKIES

INGREDIENTS:

- 4 large egg whites
- 2 cups sugar
- 1 pound slivered almonds
- 1 teaspoon vanilla extract

DIRECTIONS:

Preheat oven to 350 degrees F.

With an electric mixer, combine the egg whites and sugar and beat at a high speed until soft and creamy. Gradually add in the almonds and the vanilla extract.

Place a sheet of waxed paper on a cookie sheet. Drop teaspoons of the batter onto the waxed paper about 1 inch apart and bake until golden brown, approximately 15-20 minutes.

Remove cookies and cool on wire rack.

MINI WEDDING CAKES

MAKES APPROX. 3 DOZEN COOKIES

INGREDIENTS:

- 4 eggs
- 1 cup sugar
- 1½ cups salted butter, softened
- 2 cups all-purpose flour
- 8 ounces almond filling or paste
- 1 teaspoon almond extract
- ¼ teaspoon salt
- 12 ounces of either fig preserves, or a fruit jam – apricot, raspberry, strawberry, or prune jam, heated
- 12 ounces semisweet chocolate, melted 5 drops green food coloring
- 5 drops red food coloring
- Silver Ball, chocolate, or candy Sprinkles (optional)

DIRECTIONS:

Preheat oven to 350 degrees F.

With an electric mixing bowl beat almond filling, butter, sugar, eggs, and almond extract until the mixture is light and fluffy. Gradually add in the flour and salt. Separate the batter into 3 equal portions. Add the green food coloring to one portion and the red to another and blend into the mixture until you notice the color bleeding through evenly. Place each portion in separate bowls in the refrigerator for 10 minutes. Spread each portion with a spatula to ¼- inch thickness on separate ungreased 9 x 13-inch baking pans. Bake each layer for 12-15 minutes until lightly brown. Allow cooling before removing from pans.

Place the green layer on a cutting board, and spread evenly with the warm jam. Add the uncolored layer, and spread with the remaining warm jam. Lastly, place the red layer on top. Using a sharp knife cut the cakes into 1-inch squares and place on a wire rack with waxed paper beneath it. Pour the chocolate over the cakes and cover the tops and sides completely. Add sprinkles or cookie decorations to the tops. Place in refrigerator for 1 hour until chocolate hardens.

PIZZELLE

MAKES APPROX. 4 DOZEN COOKIES

INGREDIENTS

- 6 eggs
- 1½ cups sugar
- 1 teaspoon vanilla extract
- ¾ cup vegetable oil
- 3½ cups all-purpose baking flour
- 1½ teaspoons baking powder

**OPTIONAL:
3 TEASPOONS
OF ANISEED
(ALTHOUGH THIS IS
TRADITIONALLY USED,
I USUALLY OMIT
ANISEED, BECAUSE MY
SON LIKES THEM
BETTER THAT WAY.)**

DIRECTIONS

Preheat the Pizzelle iron.

With an electric mixer combine eggs, sugar, and oil and beat until all sugar is absorbed. Add the flour and baking powder and continue to mix. Once the batter has formed, add the vanilla extract and aniseed, if you choose.

Once the iron is hot, place a tablespoon of the batter in the center of the iron circles and close the handle. Press down for 30-40 seconds and remove Pizzelle with a fork. Place Pizzelle on cooling rack or paper towel to cool. These thicker Pizzelle are more unique and better for dipping in tea or coffee than store bought Pizzelle.

"My daughter-in-law learned that investing in a proper iron is the key to great Pizzelles. She had purchased an inexpensive iron and quickly replaced it with a traditional iron that resembled my own, which makes thicker Pizzelles." - Elisa

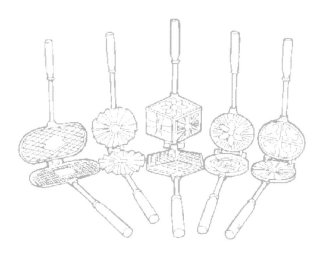

CREAM PUFFS
BIGNÉ

INGREDIENTS:

PASTRY INGREDIENTS:

- 4 large eggs
- ½ cup butter
- 1 cup water
- 1 cup all-purpose flour, sifted

CREAM FILLING:

- 6 egg yolks
- 1 quart minus 1 cup whole milk
- 12 tablespoons sugar
- 6 tablespoons all-purpose flour
- Peel of ½ lemon, whole
- 3 inches cinnamon stick

DIRECTIONS:

Preheat oven to 400 degrees F.

Prepare the Custard:

With an electric mixer, beat the egg yolks and sugar for 15 minutes. Add the flour slowly, and continue to beat at a slow speed. Pour in the milk and blend thoroughly. Pour the mixture into a medium-sized saucepan and add the cinnamon stick and lemon peel and bring to a boil over medium heat, stirring continuously. As soon as the first bubbles appear remove from heat, transfer to a glass bowl and place waxed paper directly on the surface of the filling to prevent film from forming. Chill in the refrigerator until you are ready to fill the puffs, at least 1 hour.

Prepare the Pastry:

In a medium saucepan, slowly bring water and butter to a boil. Remove from heat. With a wooden spoon beat in flour all at once. Return to heat on low and continue cooking until mixture forms a ball and leaves the sides of the pan. Remove from heat and beat in eggs, one at a time. With the wooden spoon, beat the eggs into the mixture, until the mixture is smooth and satiny and breaks into strands.

Drop by rounded tablespoons 2 inches apart onto ungreased cookie sheet and bake for 45-50 minutes until light brown or golden in color. Puffs should sound hollow when lightly tapped with fingertips. Let cool completely on wire racks away from any drafts. Now it is time to fill the puff! With a very sharp knife slice each puff in half. Drop a teaspoon of the custard, or a little more depending on your taste, and replace the lid. Once you have filled all the puffs, store in refrigerator. Sprinkle with confectioners' sugar before serving.

CREAM PUFFS
BIGNÉ

CHOCOLATE LIQUOR BISCOTTI

BISCOTTI DI CIOCCOLATO CON LIQUORE

INGREDIENTS:

- 12 eggs yolks
- 3 cups all-purpose flour, sifted
- 1½ cups sugar
- 1½ cups slivered almonds, roasted
- Zest of 1 lemon
- 1½ teaspoons baking powder
- 6 teaspoons Crisco, melted
- ½ teaspoon cinnamon
- ¼ cup Galliano Liquor, or any classic Italian yellow liquor
- 2 cups semisweet mini chocolate chips

DIRECTIONS:

Preheat oven to 350 degrees F.

Place almonds on a baking sheet and bake in oven for 10-15 minutes until lightly brown. Remove and set aside to cool. With an electric mixer, beat the egg yolks and sugar until creamy. Reduce the speed of mixer and sift in the flour and baking powder. Insert kneading or dough hook attachment and knead for 5 minutes. Add the melted Crisco, cinnamon, lemon zest, and liquor. Continue to mix for an additional five minutes. Finally, add the roasted almonds and chocolate chips.

Lightly flour a clean surface and divide the dough into 4 equal parts. Roll each part out with your hands to form a log the length of your cookie sheet and 2-3 inches wide. Line the cookie sheets with waxed paper and place 2 logs on each cookie sheet. Place in preheated oven and bake for 20 minutes. Remove from oven and allow to cool to room temperature. Cut into 1-inch diagonal strips. If you like crispy biscotti, you can return the biscotti to the oven for 5-10 minutes, then cool on wire racks.

CHOCOLATE
LIQUOR
BISCOTTI

BISCOTTI
DI CIOCCOLATO
CON LIQUORE

RICOTTA COOKIES

DOLCI DI RICOTTA

MAKES APPROX. 8 DOZEN COOKIES

INGREDIENTS

- 3 eggs
- ½ cup sugar
- 2 cups all-purpose flour
- 1 teaspoon baking powder
- 1 teaspoon baking soda
- ½ pound salted butter, softened
- 16 ounces ricotta cheese, drained
- 5 tablespoons whole milk
- 1½ cups confectioners' sugar
- 3 tablespoons vanilla extract
- ½ cup chocolate or colored candy Sprinkles

DIRECTIONS

Preheat oven to 350 degrees F.

In a mixing bowl, combine the butter, sugar, eggs, ricotta cheese, and 2 teaspoons of vanilla extract and beat until you have a creamy mixture. In a separate mixing bowl, sift the flour and add the baking powder and baking soda. Add the dry mixture to the creamy mixture and fold until you have a formed a dough. You can add a teaspoon of flour or two if mixture appears runny.

Wrap dough in clear wrap and place in refrigerator for 20 minutes. Then drop tablespoons of dough 1 inch apart on an ungreased cookie sheet. Bake for 8 to 10 minutes, until lightly browned.

While the cookies are baking, prepare the icing. With an electric mixer, beat the milk, confectioners' sugar, and 1 teaspoon of vanilla extract until smooth. Pour mixture into a glass measuring cup with a spout.

Remove cookies from the oven and place on wire racks with waxed paper under the rack. Pour the icing over the tops of the warm cookies, and add sprinkles.

SESAME COOKIES

MAKES APPROX. 7 DOZEN COOKIES

INGREDIENTS:

- 3 eggs
- 4½ to 5 cups all-purpose flour
- 1½ teaspoons baking powder
- 1 pinch salt
- ¾ cup sugar
- 2 teaspoons vanilla extract
- ½ cup salted butter, softened
- 1 cup sesame seeds
- 2 cups whole milk

DIRECTIONS:

Preheat the oven to 350 degrees F.

With an electric mixer, cream together the butter and sugar until smooth. Beat in the egg and vanilla extract until well blended. Sift the flour into the mixing bowl. Add the baking powder and salt. Let the dough mix for a few minutes to lighten the dough. The dough will be soft but should be easy to hand roll.

Pinch off pieces of dough slightly smaller than a walnut, and roll them into small logs roughly 1½ inches long. Dip in milk, and then roll in sesame seeds. Place the cookies 1-inch apart on an ungreased cookie sheet. Cookies will not spread very much. Bake for 17-20 minutes in the preheated oven, or until bottom and sides of cookies are lightly toasted. Remove from cookie sheets to cool on wire racks.

SOUR CREAM COOKIES

MAKES 6 -7 DOZEN COOKIES

INGREDIENTS:

- 4 eggs
- 6 cups all-purpose flour
- 16 ounces sour cream
- 3 cups sugar
- 1 cup Crisco
- 2 teaspoons baking powder
- 2 teaspoons baking soda
- 2 teaspoons vanilla extract

'LU CHIADRA' – COOKIE ICING

- ½ cup water
- 2 cups of confectioners' sugar
- Rainbow or Holiday Sprinkles

DIRECTIONS:

With an electric mixer, beat the eggs, sugar, and Crisco until smooth. Add the sour cream, vanilla extract, and baking soda and mix at medium speed. Finally, sift in the flour and add the baking powder. Mix for 5 minutes until all the ingredients are thoroughly blended.

Refrigerate for at least 1 hour. Preheat oven to 400 degrees F.

Spoon one tablespoon of the batter at a time onto a waxed paper-covered cookie sheet 2 inches apart because they will spread. Bake for 10-15 minutes until lightly browned; remove and cool cookies on a wire rack. In a small bowl, combine the confectioners' sugar and water, and beat with a tablespoon until mixed well. Place some waxed paper under the wire racks. Pour a tablespoon of the icing over each of the cooled cookies. Sprinkle with your favorite rainbow sprinkles. Let the icing harden before you serve or move to an airtight container.

FRIED SWEET DOUGH

CIOFFE

MAKES APPROX. 2 DOZEN CIOFFE

INGREDIENTS:

- 2 eggs
- 1 pound all-purpose flour
- 4 ounces sugar
- 2 ounces of butter, melted
- 1 pinch salt
- 2 cups vegetable oil
- ½ cup confectioners' sugar, for decoration

DIRECTIONS:

With an electric mixer, mix the flour with sugar and a pinch of salt. In a separate glass bowl, whisk the eggs and melted butter. Add the wet mixture to the flour mixture and continue to mix with the electric mixer until the dough forms. Let the dough rest for 20 minutes.

Lightly flour a clean, cold surface, and roll out the dough with a rolling pin as thin as you can make it without tearing it. Cut into strips 3 inches long by 1 inch wide. Heat the oil in a deep frying pan and drop 4-5 strips at a time into the hot oil. Using tongs, flip the cioffe until both sides are lightly golden in color. Remove from the pan, and dry on paper towel-lined wire racks. Once cool, sprinkle with confectioners' sugar and serve.

GINA'S CANDIED CHERRY COOKIES

INGREDIENTS:

- 2 egg whites
- ¼ cup all-purpose flour
- ½ cup confectioners' sugar
- ½ cup sugar
- 8 ounces almond paste
- 1 pound sliced almonds with skin
- Red and/or green candied cherries, sliced in half

DIRECTIONS:

Preheat oven to 300 degrees F.

With an electric mixer, beat the eggs and sugar at medium speed until creamy. Add the flour, confectioners' sugar, and almond paste and mix thoroughly. Spread the almonds on a plate. Take a tablespoon of dough and roll into a ball. Roll the ball through the almonds to coat.

Place the balls on an ungreased cookie sheet 1-2 inches apart. Place a half cherry centered on top of each ball and press down lightly. Bake for 20 minutes. Remove and cool on wire rack.

NUTELLA OR MARMALADE TART

CROSTATA ALLA NUTELLA O MARMELLATA

SERVES 10-12 PEOPLE

INGREDIENTS:

- 4 eggs
- 2 cups all-purpose flour
- 2 sticks of butter or margarine, softened
- 1½ cups sugar
- Zest of ½ lemon
- 26.5 ounce jar of Nutella or 2 18-ounce jars of jam or marmalade

DIRECTIONS:

Preheat oven to 350 degrees F.

With an electric mixer, beat the eggs and sugar at medium speed until creamy. Using a kneading attachment or dough hook, add the lemon zest. Gradually sift in the flour and mix for 5 minutes. Next, add the butter and knead until you have a consistent dough.

Prepare a 10–12 inch circular or rectangular tart pan with removable bottom. With a rolling pin, roll ¾ of the dough evenly on a lightly floured wooden or marble surface. Lift gently and place in the tart pan. Pat down the bottom and sides firmly to prevent rising. Poking a few holes in the dough will also ensure it does not rise. Use the remaining dough to create decorative strips for the top.

Using a spatula spread the Nutella or jam evenly in the pastry. Decorate with the strips forming a lattice. Place in the oven and bake for approximately 20-25 minutes. Remove from the oven, and set aside to cool completely. Once cool remove from pan.

NUTELLA
OR MARMALADE
TART

CROSTATA
ALLA NUTELLA
O MARMELLATA

STRAWBERRY & ITALIAN CREAM TART

CROSTATA CON FRAGOLE E CREMA

SERVES 10-12 PEOPLE

INGREDIENTS:

FOR THE PASTRY:

- 4 eggs
- 2 cups all-purpose flour
- 2 sticks butter
  or margarine, softened
- 1½ cups sugar
- Zest of ½ lemon

FOR THE CREAM:

- 6 egg yolks
- 12 tablespoons sugar
- 6 tablespoons
  all-purpose flour
- 1 quart minus one cup
  of whole milk
- Peel of ½ lemon, whole
- 3 inches cinnamon stick

FOR THE TOPPING:

- 2 cartons fresh strawberries
- ½ cup apricot jam
- 1 teaspoon lemon juice
- 1 teaspoon water

DIRECTIONS:

For the Cream:

With an electric mixer, beat the egg yolks and sugar for 15 minutes. Add the flour slowly, and continue to beat at a slow speed. Pour in the milk and blend thoroughly. Pour the mixture into a medium-sized saucepan, adding the cinnamon stick and lemon peel and bring to a boil over medium heat, stirring continuously. As soon as the first bubbles appears remove from heat, transfer to a glass bowl and place waxed paper directly on the surface of the filling to prevent film from forming. Chill in the refrigerator until you are ready to fill the tart, at least 1 hour.

Preheat oven to 350 degrees F.

For the Pastry:

With an electric mixer, beat the eggs and sugar at medium speed until creamy. Add the lemon zest, then mix. Using a kneading attachment or dough hook gradually sift in the flour and baking powder mix for 5 minutes. Add the butter to the mix and knead until you have a consistent batter.

Using your fingers, spread the dough evenly in a 10–12 inch circular or rectangular tart pan with removable bottom and pat down the bottom firmly to prevent rising. Poking a few holes in the dough will also ensure it does not rise. You may not need all the pastry. You can use the excess to make mini tarts or bocconotti cookies. Place on rack in center of oven with a dinner plate laid in the center of the tart, to keep the dough from rising. Bake for 20 minutes until pastry is lightly brown. Check to make sure the center is not rising. Remove from the oven and set aside to cool completely. Once cooled remove from pan. Remove the cream from the refrigerator and spoon evenly onto the tart.

For the Topping:

Slice the fresh strawberries in half. In a small saucepan, heat the jam, water, and lemon juice until you have a consistent mixture. Remove from heat. Arrange the strawberries cut side down in a circular pattern until the cream is completely covered. Brush the jam mixture over the strawberries and chill before serving.

STRAWBERRY & ITALIAN CREAM TART

CROSTATA CON FRAGOLE E CREMA

HONEY BALLS
OR ITALIAN DONUTS
CICERCHIATA

INGREDIENTS:

- 4 eggs
- ¼ cup salted butter
- ½ cup sugar
- 3 cups all-purpose flour
- ½ teaspoon salt
- 2 teaspoons baking powder
- 1 tablespoon lemon zest
- 2 cups oil
- 1½ cups honey
- 3 teaspoons cinnamon
- 1 teaspoon vanilla extract
- ¾ cup slivered almonds, optional
- 2 ounces silver ball or colored candy sprinkles

DIRECTIONS:

In a small mixing bowl beat the eggs. Melt the butter over low heat. Place the flour in a large mixing bowl. Add sugar, baking powder, lemon zest and salt. With your hands press the mixture to the edges of the bowl leaving a well in the middle. Pour the eggs and the melted butter into the flour mixture. Mix with a wooden spoon and then with the hands until dough leaves the sides of the bowl. Add remaining ½ cup of flour as needed. Knead dough on floured surface until it is no longer sticky.

Break off pieces of dough and roll into ropes about the size of a pencil. Cut into pieces ¼ inch long. Roll these pieces into little balls and set aside. In deep frying pan, add oil about 2 inches deep and heat. Fry balls until golden brown. Drain the balls on paper towels. In a large saucepan over medium heat, bring 1½ cups of honey to a boil. Let honey boil gently for about 3 minutes before adding little dough balls; stir gently with wooden spoon until they are well- coated.

Remove balls from honey with a slotted spoon and place in a deep dish or mound them on a platter. Sprinkle surface evenly with nuts (optional) and sprinkles.

"This is a traditional Abruzzo dessert found in almost every home during Carnevale. A wonderful centerpiece for any sweet table, or accompaniment for espresso. When your friends and neighbors pass by for the celebration, they can help themselves to as little or as much as they like. It is also the last sweet indulgence until the Easter celebration!" - Elisa

HONEY BALLS OR ITALIAN DONUTS
CICERCHIATA

ELISA'S WHISKEY CAKE

SERVES 12-15 PEOPLE

INGREDIENTS:

CAKE:

- 1 Box Butter Cake Mix & 1 Box of Instant Vanilla Pudding or 1 Box Butter Cake Mix with Pudding
- 4 eggs
- ½ cup vegetable oil
- 1 cup whole milk
- 1 shot whiskey
- 1 cup nuts, chopped

SAUCE:

- ¼ pound salted butter
- ½ cup whiskey cake
- ¾ cup sugar

DIRECTIONS:

Preheat oven to 350 degrees F.

With an electric mixer on low speed, add the eggs and the box mix. Next add the oil, milk, and whiskey. Beat for 5 minutes and add the chopped nuts. Grease a tube or Bundt pan on all sides and pour the mixture into the pan. Bake for 1 hour until lightly brown. Use a toothpick to check the center. Remove immediately from the pan and set aside on a wire rack to cool completely.

While the cake is baking, combine the butter, whiskey, and sugar for the sauce and heat in a saucepan. Once the cake has cooled, pierce the cake several times with a fork. This will allow the cake to absorb the sauce better. Pour the sauce over the cake and serve.

COFFEE CAKE
TORTA DI CAFFÉ

INGREDIENTS:

CAKE BATTER:

- 3 eggs
- 3 cups all-purpose flour
- ¾ cup butter or margarine, softened
- 1½ cups sugar
- 1½ teaspoons baking powder
- 1½ teaspoons baking soda
- ½ teaspoon salt
- 1½ cups sour cream
- 1½ teaspoons vanilla extract

FILLING:

- ½ cup of dark brown sugar, packed
- ½ cup finely chopped nuts
- 1½ teaspoons cinnamon
- 1 shot espresso coffee

DIRECTIONS:

Preheat oven to 350 degrees F.

With an electric mixer, beat the eggs and sugar at medium speed. Add the butter or margarine and vanilla extract and continue beating at medium speed for 2 minutes. Sift the flour into the mixture and add the baking powder, baking soda, salt and sour cream. Mix thoroughly and set aside. In a separate mixing bowl, using a wooden spoon, mix the brown sugar, nuts, cinnamon and coffee, until you have a consistent mixture.

Grease the bottom and sides of a tube or Bundt pan and pour ⅓ of the batter into the pan. Sprinkle ⅓ of the filling mixture into the batter. Add another ⅓ of the batter and sprinkle with another ⅓ of the filling. Finally, add the remaining batter and sprinkle with the remaining filling on top. Bake for 60 minutes until lightly brown. Test with a toothpick in the center to make sure batter is cooked thoroughly. Remove from pan and cool on a wire rack.

RUM MOSTACCIOLI COOKIES

MAKES APPROX. 9 DOZEN COOKIES

INGREDIENTS:

- 32 egg yolks
- 8 cups flour
- 5 cups sugar
- 32 ounces dark chocolate, melted
- 6 cups chopped almonds
- 1 cup rum
- 7 teaspoons cinnamon
- 2 zest of lemons
- ½ cup unsweetened cocoa powder
- 3 cups honey
- 2 teaspoons vanilla extract

DIRECTIONS:

Preheat oven to 350 degrees F.

Place almonds on a baking sheet in a single layer and roast evenly until lightly brown. Do not allow them to burn. Chop after they have cooled.

With an electric mixer, beat egg yolks and sugar together. Gradually add the flour and melted chocolate. Continue beating and add the almonds, cinnamon, lemon zest, cocoa powder, honey, and vanilla extract. Finally add the rum.

Grease a flat surface with some olive oil and place batter on greased surface. If the batter is sticking, brush the top of the batter with additional olive oil. Roll the dough to ¼-inch thickness. Cut rows of dough into 1½ -inch wide rows, then into individual slanted rectangles 3 inches long. Place cookies on a greased cookie sheet 1-inch apart and bake in preheated oven for 12-15 minutes. Remove from oven and cool on wire racks.

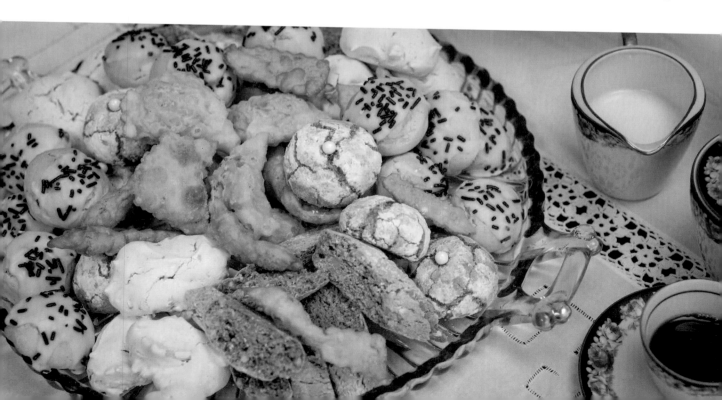

WALNUT COOKIES
DOLCETTI DI NOCE

INGREDIENTS:

- 3 eggs
- 3 cups all-purpose flour
- 1½ cups sugar
- 2½ cups walnuts, pieces
- 1 tablespoon cocoa powder
- 1 teaspoon baking powder
- Silver candy decorating balls, optional

DIRECTIONS:

Preheat oven to 350 degrees F.

With an electric mixer, beat the egg and sugar until creamy. Reduce the speed and sift in the flour, cocoa, and baking powder. Insert your kneading or dough hook attachment and knead for 5 minutes. Add the walnuts and continue to mix for an additional five minutes until you have a consistent dough.

You can shape these cookies in two fashions:

Long - Lightly flour a clean surface and divide the dough into 4 equal parts. Roll each part out with your hands to form a log the length of your cookie sheet and 2 inches wide. Line the cookie sheets with waxed paper and place 2 logs on each cookie sheet.

Round – Pinch a walnut-sized portion of dough and roll into a ball with your hands; place on a waxed paper-covered cookie sheet and press down gently. Add one silver-decorating ball to the center.

Both methods require a cooking time of 15-20 minutes. Remove from oven and cool on a wire rack. For the logs, once they have cooled to room temperature, cut diagonally into 2-inch

CANNOLI
CAKE

TORTA
DI CANNOLI

INGREDIENTS

FOR THE CAKE:

- 3 cups all-purpose flour
- 3½ teaspoons baking powder
- ½ teaspoon salt
- ¾ cup unsalted butter, softened
- 1½ cups sugar
- 6 large egg yolks
- 1 cup whole milk
- 2 teaspoons vanilla extract

NOTE – IN A RUSH, YOU CAN USE A BOX OF BUTTER CAKE MIX.

FOR THE FILLING:

- 16 ounces ricotta cheese
- ½ cup confectioners' sugar
- 2 teaspoons ground cinnamon
- ½ teaspoon almond extract
- 1 teaspoon rum
- 1 teaspoon vanilla extract
- ½ cup semisweet chocolate, finely chopped or mini chocolate chips

FOR THE FROSTING:

- 16 ounces mascarpone cheese
- 1 cup confectioners' sugar
- ¼ cup whole milk
- 3 teaspoons vanilla extract

FOR THE GARNISH:

- 2 cups mini chocolate chips
- 2 cannoli shells

DIRECTIONS

Preheat oven to 350 degrees F.

Prepare the Cakes:

Grease two 9-inch cake pans with butter and flour. In a bowl sift or whisk the flour with the baking powder and salt. With an electric mixer, beat the butter until soft and creamy.

Gradually add the sugar. Add egg yolks, in two batches, beating well after each addition. Scrape the sides of the bowl as needed. Finally, add the vanilla extract and beat until combined.

On low speed, gradually add the flour mixture and milk, alternating between the two, beginning and ending with the flour. Evenly divide the batter between the prepared pans. Bake 20-25 minutes. Insert a toothpick into the center of the cake to confirm the center is cooked. Remove from the oven and place the cakes, in their pans, on a wire rack to cool for about 10 minutes. Then remove the cakes from pans onto the rack. Allow the cakes to cool before frosting.

Prepare the Filling:

In a large bowl, combine the ricotta cheese, confectioners' sugar, cinnamon, rum, and almond and vanilla extract. Stir in chocolate with a wooden spoon. Refrigerate until ready to use.

Prepare the Frosting:

With an electric mixer, beat the mascarpone cheese, confectioners' sugar, and vanilla extract on medium speed. Gradually add the milk until the mixture is thick and creamy.

Assemble the Cake:

Place one cake layer on a serving plate; spread the filling evenly over the cake. Top with the second cake layer. Frost the sides and top of the cake with the mascarpone frosting. Line the sides of the cake with the chocolate chips and press gently so they stick to the frosting. Using an icing bag and large nozzle, drop circles of frosting, 1 inch in diameter, around the top and bottom of the cake. Garnish the center with the mini chocolate chips and the filled cannoli shells, refrigerate until you are ready to serve.

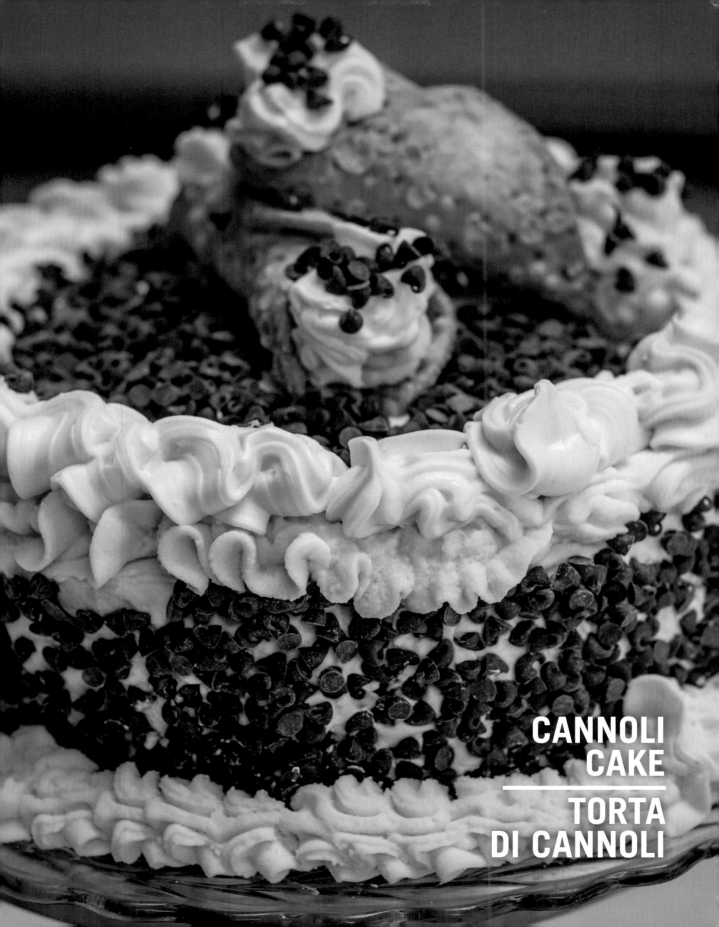

CANNOLI CAKE

TORTA DI CANNOLI

PASQUALINA'S COOKIES

"This recipe was given to me by a dear friend of mine, whom I had the pleasure of working alongside in the kitchen at Divine Providence for 8 years." – Elisa

In loving memory of Pasqualina Duranti
1933– 2012

INGREDIENTS

- 12 egg yolks
- 2 egg whites
- 5 cups all-purpose flour
- 2 cups sugar
- 2 cups slivered almonds, roasted
- 1 teaspoon cinnamon
- 1 teaspoon baking powder
- ½ cup mixed liquor, whiskey, rum, and coffee liquors
- 1 tablespoon Crisco
- 1 bar of dark baking chocolate, melted
- Confectioners' sugar

DIRECTIONS

Preheat oven to 350 degrees F.

Place almonds on a baking sheet and toast in oven for 10-15 minutes until lightly brown. Remove and set aside to cool. In a small saucepan melt the chocolate and Crisco, stirring continuously to avoid burning. Remove from heat and set aside.

With an electric mixer, beat the egg whites and sugar for 3 minutes and then add the egg yolks and continue beating for 5 minutes. Sift the flour into the mixture, then using a kneading attachment or dough hook, knead for 5 minutes. Add the baking powder, almonds, cinnamon, and liquor and continue kneading for 5 minutes. Finally, pour the melted chocolate into the mixer and knead until well blended.

Drop dough by the tablespoon onto a waxed paper-covered cookie sheet and bake for 10-15 minutes. Remove from the oven and cool on a wire rack. Once cool, sift confectioners' sugar over the tops and serve.

CIAMBELLONE

INGREDIENTS:

- 8 eggs
- 2¼ cups sugar
- 3½ cups all-purpose flour
- 1 cup vegetable oil
- 2 teaspoons baking powder
- 1 cup mini chocolate chips, optional

DIRECTIONS:

Preheat oven to 350 degrees F.

In a large mixing bowl, beat the eggs and sugar until creamy and blend thoroughly. Add the oil and mix. Finally add the flour, baking powder, and chocolate chips. Grease and flour a tube baking pan. Pour in the batter. Sprinkle the top of the batter with additional sugar and bake in the oven for 1 hour. Test the center of the cake with toothpick. If the toothpick comes out clean, the cake is fully cooked. Remove cake from the pan and cool on a wire rack.

PEACHES

PESCHE DOLCI

MAKES APPROX. 2 DOZEN PEACHES

INGREDIENTS

FOR THE COOKIES:

- 3 large eggs
- 2 cups sugar
- 1 cup vegetable oil
- 1 teaspoon vanilla extract
- 4 teaspoons baking powder
- ½ teaspoon salt
- 1 cup whole milk
- 6 cups all-purpose flour

FOR THE CREAM:

- 6 egg yolks
- 1 quart minus 1 cup whole milk
- 12 tablespoons sugar
- 6 tablespoons all-purpose flour
- Peel of ½ lemon
- 3 inches cinnamon stick

FOR DECORATING:

- 2 cups Peach Liqueur
- 3 drops yellow food coloring
- 3 drops red food coloring
- Crystal sugar
- Mint Leaves, for garnish

DIRECTIONS

Preheat oven to 350 degrees F.

For the Cream:

With an electric mixer beat the egg yolks and sugar for 15 minutes. Add the flour slowly and continue to beat at a low speed. Pour in the milk and blend thoroughly. Pour the mixture into a medium-sized saucepan, then add the cinnamon stick and lemon peel. Bring to a boil over medium heat, stirring continuously. As soon as the first bubbles appear, remove from heat and transfer to a glass bowl. Place waxed paper directly on the surface of the filling to prevent film from forming. Chill in the refrigerator until you are ready to fill, at least 1 hour.

For the Cookies:

Line two baking sheets with waxed paper. With an electric mixer, beat the eggs and sugar for about 3 minutes until light. Add the oil and beat until creamy. Mix in ¾ of the milk and vanilla. In a small bowl beat the baking powder with the remaining milk. Add along with the flour to the batter and beat until you have an even consistency. Take a small amount of batter in your hands and roll into a ball approximately 1½ inches in diameter. Place these on the baking sheets 2 inches apart. The cookies will spread during baking. Bake the cookies for about 15-20 minutes or until very light brown on the bottom. Remove from the oven and cool on wire racks. Once cool, scoop out the center of the cookie from the bottom with a spoon, being careful not to break the top outer shell of the cookie.

How to Decorate:

Divide the 2 cups of peach liqueur into two separate bowls, deep enough to submerge the peaches. Add 3 drops of yellow food coloring to one bowl and mix. Add 3 drops of red food coloring to the other bowl and mix. In a third bowl, place the sugar. Carefully dip each cookie into the red mixture ¾ of the way up the peach. Shake gently and dip the other end in the yellow mixture. Gently blot the cookie with paper towels to remove most of the liquid, then immediately roll the cookie in the sugar. Place the finished cookie on a sheet of waxed paper to dry. Place a tablespoon of cream into the center of one cookie and seal with another cookie. Insert a couple of mint leaves to resemble the leaves of a peach. Refrigerate until you are ready to serve.

PEACHES
___
PESCHE
DOLCI

CHOCOLATE CAKE

TORTA CIOCCOLATA

SERVES 8–10 PEOPLE

INGREDIENTS:

- 2 large eggs
- 2 cups all-purpose flour
- 1½ cups sugar
- 2 teaspoons baking powder
- 2 teaspoons baking soda
- ¾ cup cocoa powder
- ¾ cup vegetable oil
- 1 cup whole milk or heavy cream
- 1 cup hot espresso coffee
- 1 teaspoon vanilla extract
- Confectioners' sugar,
  for decorating

DIRECTIONS:

Preheat oven to 350 degrees F.

Grease a tube or Bundt pan. With an electric mixer, beat the eggs and sugar until creamy. Sift in the flour and add the baking powder, baking soda and vanilla extract; mix for 5 minutes.

Add the cocoa, oil, and milk and continue to mix for 5 minutes. Finally, add the coffee and beat for an additional 2 minutes. Pour the batter into the tube or Bundt pan and bake in the oven for 40-45 minutes.

Use a toothpick to check the center. Remove immediately from the pan and set aside on a wire rack to cool completely.

ITALIAN RUM CAKE

"This is a classic celebration cake, and one of my daughter Nadia's favorites. I make this every year on her birthday." - Elisa

INGREDIENTS

FOR THE CAKE:

- 9 eggs
- 1½ cups sugar
- 2 cups all-purpose flour
- 2 teaspoons baking powder
- 3 cups dark rum, for assembly of cake
- 3 cups nuts, chopped or almonds, sliced, for assembly of cake

BUTTER CREAM FROSTING:

- 6 cups confectioners' sugar
- 2 cups salted butter, softened
- 8 tablespoons whipping cream
- 4 teaspoons vanilla extract

FOR THE ITALIAN CREAM:

- 6 egg yolks
- 12 tablespoons sugar
- 6 tablespoons all-purpose flour
- 3½ cups whole milk
- 3 inches cinnamon stick
- Peel of ½ a lemon, whole

WHIPPED CREAM FROSTING:

- 2 cups heavy cream
- 3 tablespoons confectioners' sugar
- 1 teaspoon vanilla extract

FOR THE CHOCOLATE CREAM:

- 6 egg yolks
- 12 tablespoons sugar
- 6 tablespoons all-purpose flour
- 3½ cups whole milk
- 3 inches cinnamon stick
- Peel of ½ a lemon, whole
- 1 bag of unsweetened chocolate chips
- 8 tablespoons whipping cream

DIRECTIONS:

Preheat oven to 325 degrees F.

Prepare the batter with an electric mixer. Beat the egg at high speed and gradually add in the sugar until creamy. Reduce the speed and continue mixing while sifting in the flour and baking powder. Beat until batter is consistent.

Grease the sides and bottom of two 9-inch round cake pans. Divide the batter equally between the two pans and bake for 1 hour. Once baked, remove from pans and cool on a wire rack.

With an electric mixer beat the egg yolks and sugar for 15 minutes. Add the flour slowly and continue to beat at a low speed. Pour in the milk and blend thoroughly. Pour the mixture into a medium-sized saucepan, then add the cinnamon stick and lemon peel. Bring to a boil over medium heat, stirring continuously. As soon as the first bubbles appear, remove from heat and transfer to a glass bowl. Place waxed paper directly on the surface of the filling to prevent film from forming. Chill in the refrigerator until you are ready to use, at least 1 hour.

Follow the steps for the Italian cream to prepare the chocolate cream as well. Once you remove the cream from the heat, remove the cinnamon and lemon peel, and stir in the chocolate chips thoroughly until all the chips have melted. Transfer to a glass bowl. Place waxed paper directly on the surface of the filling to prevent film from forming. Chill in the refrigerator until you are ready to assemble the cake, at least 1 hour.

For Butter Cream Frosting, beat the butter at high speed with an electric mixer until fluffy. Add the confectioners' sugar and beat at medium speed until well mixed. Add vanilla extract, and cream. Blend on low until the mixture is smooth. Increase the speed to high, and beat until the icing is fluffy.

For the Whipped Cream Frosting, beat the heavy cream at high speed in an electric mixer and gradually add sugar and vanilla extract. Continue to beat until light and fluffy. Cool in refrigerator until ready to use.

To Assemble the Cake:

Cut both cake layers in half horizontally. Place one of the layers, cut side up, on the cake dish or pedestal. Brush some of the rum over the cake; do not oversoak the cake. Spread half of Italian cream evenly on the cake. Add a second layer of cake, cut side up. Brush some of the rum over the cake and spread the chocolate cream on the cake. Add the third layer of cake, cut side up. Brush some of the rum on the cake and spread the remaining Italian cream evenly on the cake. Top with the final layer of cake, cut side down.

Using a spatula, ice the cake with the frosting you have chosen to use. For whipped cream frosting, decorate the top with some nuts or jimmies and refrigerate until ready to serve. For butter cream frosting, frost the entire cake with a layer of the butter cream frosting, add the remaining frosting to a pastry bag with a closed star tip and refrigerate the frosting until ready to use.

Take some nuts or almonds in the palm of your hand, and gently press the nuts along the side of the cake from top to bottom. Take the piping bag out of the refrigerator and use in a circular motion to make roses around the top, making them large enough to meet the nuts.

Add 3 roses to the top.

"You have two choices. If you are an experienced cake decorator, I recommend the butter cream because it is easier for piping flowers. If you want a simpler appearance, frosting with the whipped cream is easy and quick. Make sure you allow time for the rum to settle in the cake and refrigerate immediately after frosting it. Another option is to frost the cake with the remaining chocolate cream." - Elisa

ITALIAN
RUM CAKE

CHERRY RICOTTA PIE

SERVES 6-8 PEOPLE

INGREDIENTS:

- 6 eggs
- 3 pounds ricotta cheese, drained well
- 1 cup sugar
- ¼ cup whiskey
- 10-12 ounces maraschino cherries
- 3 cups butter cookies, finely chopped

DIRECTIONS:

Preheat oven to 350 degrees F.

Using a food processer or blender, chop the butter cookies until they are very fine. You can also use graham crackers or a store-bought graham cracker piecrust. Line the bottom and sides of a 9-inch pie pan with the chopped cookies to form a crust. Refrigerate while you prepare the filling.

In a large mixing bowl, whisk the eggs and gradually add in the sugar and continue to whisk. Fold in the ricotta cheese until you have a consistent mixture. Finally, add the whiskey and blend through. Remove the piecrust from the refrigerator and fill with the mixture. Bake for 1 hour. Remove from oven and cool on a wire rack. Cracking is normal. If you want to decorate this pie, I recommend you use a whipped cream icing and decorate the edges and center.

Garnish with a few cherries.

ITALIAN CHRISTMAS NOUGAT
TORRONE

INGREDIENTS

- 1 cup honey
- 2 egg whites
- 1 cup sugar
- 2 tablespoons water
- 1 pound almond slivers
- ½ teaspoon lemon zest
- ½ pound hazelnuts, slightly toasted
- 1 teaspoon candied orange, peeled and chopped
- Rice Paper Wafers

DIRECTIONS

Place honey on top of double boiler over boiling water and stir with a wooden spoon for at least 1 hour until the honey is caramelized. Beat the egg whites until stiff and add to the honey slowly and blend thoroughly. The mixture should become fluffy and white in color. In a separate small saucepan, combine the sugar and water and boil until caramelized.

Gradually add to the honey mixture and blend thoroughly. Cook for an additional five minutes. The temperature should read 315 Degrees F on a candy thermometer. Remove from heat and add the almonds, hazelnuts, candied oranges and mix thoroughly.

Lightly grease the sides of a 9 x 13-inch baking sheet. Line the bottom with wafer paper, touching at sides but not overlapping, and set aside. Pour the mixture into prepared pan and cover with another layer of wafer paper. Let cool for 20 minutes. Remove from the pan and cut with into 1-inch by 2-inch rectangular bars. Let cool completely.

DEEP FRIED CHESTNUT RAVIOLI
CAGGIONETTI

INGREDIENTS:

FOR THE FILLING:

- ¼ cup of Espresso coffee, twice brewed
- ½ cup of whiskey
- Zest of 1 lemon
- 1½ cups almonds, roasted & crushed
- 1 cup sugar
- 1 tablespoon cocoa powder
- 1 cup mini chocolate chips, crushed
- 16-ounce jar dry chestnuts, crushed
- 1 teaspoon ground cinnamon

FOR THE DOUGH:

- 3 cups all-purpose flour
- 1 cup white wine
- ½ cup vegetable oil

DIRECTIONS:

Preheat oven to 400 degrees F. Place the almonds on a cookie sheet and bake in the oven for 4-6 minutes until lightly golden. Once cooled, crush almonds. In a medium-sized bowl combine all the filling ingredients and mix thoroughly with your hands. You can use a food processor or blender to crush the almonds, chestnuts and chocolate chips. Refrigerate until ready to use.

Preheat 2 cups of vegetable oil in a medium saucepan. Make a mound of flour and hollow out a well in the center. Add the wine and oil to the well and blend in the flour with a fork. Once the flour and liquids have blended, begin to knead the dough to an even consistency. Roll the dough into a thin sheet with a pasta machine or lightly floured rolling pin. Put a tablespoon of the filling in the center of the dough leaving 1 inch between each drop of filling. Fold over the dough and cut with a wheel cutter, just like ravioli. Press the ends tightly to avoid opening during frying.

Drop the pastry in the oil and fry on each side for 30 seconds. Remove from oil with a slotted spoon and place on a paper towel-covered wire rack for cooling. Sprinkle with confectioners' sugar before serving.

DEEP FRIED
CHESTNUT
RAVIOLI
CAGGIONETTI

SNOWBALLS
PALLE DI NEVE

MAKES APPROX. 3 DOZEN

INGREDIENTS:

- 1 cup all-purpose flour
- 2 tablespoons sugar
- 2 tablespoons light brown sugar
- ½ cup unsalted butter, softened
- 1 teaspoon vanilla extract
- ½ cup walnuts or pecans, chopped
- 2 cups confectioners' sugar

DIRECTIONS:

Preheat oven to 350 degrees F.

With an electric mixer, knead the flour and butter for 5 minutes. Add the sugars and vanilla extract; continue to knead for 5 minutes until dough forms. Remove the mixing bowl from the mixer, add in the nuts and mix with a wooden spoon. Place the dough in the refrigerator and chill for at least 1 hour.

Remove from the refrigerator and form into balls the size of walnuts and place on an ungreased cookie sheet 1 inch apart. Bake for 15 minutes. Remove balls from the oven and cool on a wire rack. Place the confectioners' sugar in a large plastic bag, place 3-4 balls in the bag and shake until covered completely with sugar. Transfer snowballs to a plate or air-tight container until ready to serve.

CHOCOLATE NOUGAT
TORRONE DI CIOCCOLATA

INGREDIENTS:

- ½ cup honey
- 2 egg whites
- 1 cup sugar
- 2 tablespoons water
- 1½ pounds hazelnuts, lightly toasted
- 8 squares bitter chocolate
- Rice Paper Wafers

DIRECTIONS:

Place honey on top of double boiler over boiling water and stir with a wooden spoon for at least 1 hour until the honey is caramelized. Beat the egg whites until stiff and add to the honey slowly and blend thoroughly. The mixture should become fluffy and white in color.

In a separate small saucepan, combine the sugar and water and boil until caramelized. Add gradually to the honey mixture and blend thoroughly. Add the chocolate squares and cook all together stirring continuously until all the chocolate has melted and is thoroughly blended.

The temperature should read 315 degrees F on a candy thermometer. Remove from heat and add the hazelnuts and mix.

Lightly grease the sides of a 9 x 13-inch baking sheet. Line the bottom with wafer paper, touching at sides but not overlapping and set aside. Pour the mixture into prepared pan and cover with another layer of wafer paper. Let cool for 20 minutes. Remove from the pan and cut with into rectangular bars 1 inch by 2 inches. Let cool completely.

GINA'S CHOCOLATE AMARETTO COOKIES

DOLCI DI GINA ALL' AMARETTO E CIOCCOLATA

MAKES APPROX. 2 DOZEN COOKIES

INGREDIENTS:

- 4 eggs
- 1½ cups sugar
- 3 cups all-purpose flour
- 2 teaspoons vanilla extract
- 2 teaspoons baking powder
- ½ cup cocoa powder
- ½ cup vegetable oil
- ½ cup Amaretto liquor or rum
- ½ cup confectioners' sugar

DIRECTIONS:

Preheat oven to 350 degrees F.

In a large metal bowl, add the eggs, sugar, flour, vanilla extract, cocoa, liquor and mix with a wooden spoon. In a separate bowl, mix together the oil and confectioners' sugar.

Grease your hands with the oil from the bowl, take a teaspoon full of dough and roll into a ball. Drop the ball into the confectioners' sugar and place on a greased cookie sheet. Arrange the balls 1 inch apart on the cookie sheet. Bake for 15 minutes. Remove from the oven and cool on a wire rack.

HAZELNUT BALLS

MAKES APPROX. 2 DOZEN COOKIES

INGREDIENTS:

- ½ cup butter or margarine, softened
- 2 tablespoons sugar
- 1 cup all-purpose flour
- 1 cup hazelnuts, finely chopped
- 2 teaspoons vanilla extract
- ½ teaspoon salt
- ½ cup confectioners' sugar

DIRECTIONS:

Preheat oven to 375 degrees F.

In a large metal bowl, add the butter, sugar, flour, vanilla extract, and hazelnuts and mix with your hands to form a soft dough. Wrap the dough with plastic wrap and refrigerate for 30 minutes. Add the confectioners' sugar to a bowl.

Take 1½ teaspoons of dough and roll into a ball. Arrange the balls 1-inch apart on an ungreased cookie sheet. Bake for 15–20 minutes. Cookies must set but not brown. Remove from the oven and cool on a wire rack. Allow to sit for 2-3 minutes, then roll the balls in the confectioners' sugar while still warm.

Return the balls to the wire rack. Prior to serving, roll the balls in the confectioners' sugar a second time .

WALNUT JELLY COOKIES

BISCOTTI DI NOCE E GELATINA

MAKES APPROX. 2 DOZEN COOKIES

INGREDIENTS:

- 1 egg white
- 1 egg yolk
- 1 cup all-purpose flour
- ¼ pound butter, softened
- ⅓ cup sugar
- 1 teaspoon vanilla extract
- 1 teaspoon almond extract
- ¼ tablespoon salt
- 3 ounces walnuts, chopped
- 9 ounces strawberry, raspberry, or blackberry jelly

DIRECTIONS:

Preheat oven to 325 degrees F.

With an electric mixer beat the butter for 2 minutes, until fluffy. Add the egg yolk, vanilla, almond extract, salt and continue to beat. On low speed add the flour and beat until thoroughly blended.

Beat the egg white in a separate bowl until fluffy. Place the walnuts in a separate bowl. Scoop about 2 teaspoons of dough and roll into a ball in the palms of your hands. Dip each ball into the egg whites and then roll in the walnuts. Place the balls on a waxed paper-covered cookie sheet and press the centers of the balls down with your thumb to form a small well. Add ½ teaspoon of your chosen jelly in each well. Bake for 15 minutes.

Remove from the oven and cool on a wire rack.

"My good friend Gina Tulli, came to America and settled in Philadelphia as a teenager. She made the journey alone, leaving her mother and siblings behind in Sicily. She was one of the thousands of Italians granted asylum during the war when their homes and lives were destroyed. We belonged to the same parish, St. Callistus in West Philadelphia, and our daughters attended the same school. I would see her at school functions and we greeted each other with a friendly smile. Her daughter, Anna Marie, was one of the only children who would sit on the bench with my daughter Agnes, because of her leg braces, while the other children played. We moved to Newtown Square, and I never thought much about her or my old neighborhood again. It would be years later that we became great friends.

On my first day of work at Don Guanella, I recognized her smiling face in the hallway, and she mine. We talked, and I shared with her that Agnes had passed away. From that day forward Gina took me under her wing at work and always reminded me what a happy child Agnes was. Gina is an excellent baker, and throughout the years has shared many recipes with me. On many occasions, she has worked alongside me to prepare dozens and dozens of these Italian specialties, including the 60-foot-long dessert table at my daughter's wedding.

She was the first person to whom we mentioned the idea of this book, and she pushed us continuously to start it and to finish it. She is a true friend, and I am so grateful that even though I missed the first opportunity to befriend her, God gave me a second chance." - Elisa

APPLE BUTTER COOKIES

INGREDIENTS:

FOR THE FILLING:

- 28 ounces apple butter
- 10 ounces peach preserves
- ¼ cup all-purpose flour
- 1½ cups almonds, roasted and crushed
- 2 teaspoons cocoa powder
- 1 ounce rum
- 1 lemon peel, grated
- 1 orange peel, grated

FOR THE DOUGH:

- 6 eggs
- 1 cup sugar
- ¼ cup milk
- 1 teaspoon vanilla extract
- 1 tablespoon lemon juice
- 5 teaspoons baking powder
- 8 ounces Crisco
- 5 cups all-purpose flour

DIRECTIONS:

Preheat oven to 350 degrees F.

Arrange the crushed almonds evenly on a cookie sheet, place in preheated oven, and roast for 4-6 minutes. Remove from the oven.

Prepare the filling: In a small saucepan over low heat, cook the apple butter and flour until blended thoroughly. Remove from heat and transfer to glass mixing bowl. Add the peach preserves, almonds, cocoa, rum, lemon, and orange. Mix thoroughly with a wooden spoon and set aside.

Prepare the dough: In a large mixing bowl, beat the eggs by hand. You can also use an electric mixer. Add in the sugar, milk, vanilla extract, lemon juice, baking powder, flour, and Crisco and mix thoroughly with a wooden spoon. For electric mixers, you will need to change to the kneading attachment. On a lightly floured wooden or marble surface, roll out the dough with a rolling pin to form a rectangular sheet of dough about ⅛ thick.

Spread the apple butter mixture evenly over the dough with a spatula. Roll the dough like a jellyroll. Place on a waxed paper-covered cookie sheet and bake for 20 minutes. Remove and cool on a wire rack. Slice the roll into 1- to 1½ -inch slices.

RICOTTA CHEESECAKE

TORTA DI RICOTTA

SERVES 10-12 PEOPLE

INGREDIENTS:

- 3 pounds whole ricotta cheese, well drained
- 2 cups sugar
- 8 eggs, separated
- ½ cup all-purpose flour
- 1 teaspoon vanilla extract
- ½ cup heavy cream
- ½ tablespoon lemon zest, grated
- 2 cups graham crackers, crushed

DIRECTIONS:

Preheat oven to 425 degrees F.

Grease the sides and bottom of a 12-inch Springform pan.

You can also prepare this in a 13 x 9 x 2-inch glass casserole dish. Line the bottom and sides of the pan with the crushed graham crackers. Separate the eggs.

With an electric mixer, slowly beat the drained ricotta until creamy. Gradually add ¾ of the sugar and all the egg yolks and continue to beat until well blended. Sift in the flour, then add the lemon rind and vanilla extract. Continue to mix at a low speed.

In a separate mixing bowl, beat the heavy cream, then add the egg whites and sugar, mixing thoroughly. At low speed add the heavy cream mixture to the ricotta. Increase speed and blend thoroughly. Pour the mixture into prepared pan. Bake for 10 minutes. Reduce the oven temperature to 350 degrees F and continue to bake for 1 hour. Remove cake from oven and allow to cool. Cake may be served chilled or at room temperature.

RICOTTA CAKE

FIATONE DI RICOTTA

SERVES 8-10 PEOPLE

INGREDIENTS

FOR THE FILLING:

- 10 eggs, separated
- 2½ pounds ricotta cheese
- 10 tablespoons sugar
- Zest of 1 lemon

FOR THE PASTRY:

- 3 eggs
- 3½ cups all-purpose flour
- 4 tablespoons vegetable oil
- 3 tablespoons sugar
- 2 teaspoons baking powder
- 1 teaspoon lemon juice

DIRECTIONS

Wrap and drain the ricotta in cloth. Refrigerate for 12 hours, changing the wet cloth at least twice. In a small bowl, beat the egg whites. With an electric mixer, beat the egg yolks and sugar until creamy, then add the grated lemon zest. Reduce the electric mixer speed to low and gradually fold in the egg whites. Finally, add the ricotta cheese to the mixer and blend until thoroughly combined. Refrigerate until you have finished preparing the pastry. Grease a large tube cake pan with a large center opening and preheat the oven to 325 degrees F.

On a clean wooden or marble-like surface, form a mound of flour. Dig out a well in the center and add the eggs. Beat the eggs with a fork. Add the oil, lemon juice, sugar, baking powder, and blend in with the eggs. Begin to blend in the flour with the egg mixture, then work with your hands to form a dough. Roll out the dough with a rolling pin twice the size of your pan base. Loosely lay the dough over the top of your pan and pinch the center top of the dough. Cut with scissors so it falls into your pan covering the sides and the outer sides of the center pipe of your pan. Remove the filling from the refrigerator, and spoon into the pan. You should have excess dough hanging over all the sides of the pan. Fold over the dough to cover the top of the mixture. Pinch the dough to securely seal the joints of the dough around the center tube. It will resemble a large Chinese dumpling. Place in the oven and bake for 2 hours. Gently remove from pan and turn over onto a wire rack to cool.

MINI PIE COOKIES

BOCCONOTTI

DEPENDING ON TARTLETS, MAKES 2-3½ DOZEN COOKIES

INGREDIENTS:

FOR THE PASTRY:

- 6 eggs
- 8 cups all-purpose flour
- 3 sticks butter or margarine
- 1½ cups sugar
- Zest of 1 lemon
- 6 teaspoons baking powder

FOR CHOCOLATE FILLING:

- ½ cup slivered almonds
- 2 eggs whites
- 2 tablespoons cocoa powder
- Pinch of cinnamon
- ½ teaspoon vanilla extract
- 2 ounces bitter dark baking chocolate
- ¼ cup sugar

FOR FRUIT FILLING:

The sky is the limit. You can use any flavor of jam you like: blackberry, grape, fig, prune, apricot, strawberry, apple butter, or for a yummy chocolate taste, Nutella.

Mini tartlet pans, 1½ by ¾-inch recommended, for variation. Or use some 4.75-inch round tart or quiche pans

DIRECTIONS:

For the Pastry:

On a clean wooden or marble-like surface, form a mound with the flour. Dig out a well in the center and add the eggs. Beat the eggs with a fork. Add the sugar, lemon zest, and baking powder and blend in with the eggs. Cut the butter into very small cubes. Begin to blend in the flour with the egg mixture, adding pieces of the butter. Begin to knead with your hands, adding more butter cubes and continue to work with your hands to form dough. Wrap the dough in plastic wrap and refrigerate for at least 1 hour. You can also use an electric mixer with a kneading attachment.

For the chocolate filling:

Place all the dry ingredients in a food processor or blender and grind them until you have a fine powder. In a separate bowl, beat the egg whites until stiff peaks form. Gradually fold in the dry ingredients into the egg whites. Finally, add the vanilla extract and mix it through. Preheat the oven to 350 degrees F.

Assemble your cookies:

Take a healthy tablespoon full of dough and roll between the palms of your hands to form a ball. Place the ball of dough in the center of the tartlet form and using your fingers press it into the tartlet mold so that it covers the bottom and edges equally. Trim excess dough. Add a tablespoon of the filling to the tartlet. Now, here are some options; you can leave some tartlets open-faced, or cover them like a pie. To cover, take another ball between your palms, and roll it out with a rolling pin. Place the rolled out dough over the filling and pinch the ends to seal the dough around the edges. Break off excess dough.

For the 4.75-inch quiche pans, make balls with 2 tablespoons of dough, and roll out some dough for the top. Use a cutting wheel to cut small strips and place them like lattice over the filling, pinching off the ends to seal with the bottom layer of dough.

Place all the filled tartlets atop a cookie sheet and bake 18-20 minutes until the dough is lightly browned. Cool on a rack. When cool remove the bocconotti from the tartlet forms. You can decorate by dusting with powdered sugar.

"This recipe was the specialty of one of my first neighbors and best of friends. We shared many a cup of coffee talking and raising our families together. She was one of the most elegant ladies I have ever met." - Elisa

In loving memory of Elena Riccione
1948 - 2013

TIRAMISU

INGREDIENTS:

- 1 16-ounce package ladyfinger cookies
- 5 eggs, separated
- 5 tablespoons sugar, plus 4 tablespoons
- 16 ounces mascarpone cheese
- 2 ounces Kahlua liquor, plus 3 tablespoons
- 6 cups espresso coffee, cooled
- Unsweetened cocoa powder, for garnishing

DIRECTIONS:

Prepare your espresso coffee and set aside to cool. Separate the eggs and beat the egg whites in a mixing bowl until stiff. With an electric mixer, beat the egg yolks with 5 tablespoons of sugar until creamy. Fold in the mascarpone into the egg yolk mixture, then add 2 ounces of Kahlua. At a low speed, fold in the egg whites.

Place a light layer of the mascarpone mixture in the bottom of a 11 x 9 x 2-inch glass casserole pan. Mix the cooled coffee with the remaining sugar and Kahlua. Dip each ladyfinger lightly into the coffee mixture and line tightly in the pan. Add a layer of the mascarpone mixture and sprinkle with the cocoa powder. Add a second layer of dipped ladyfingers, mascarpone mixture and cocoa. Refrigerate until ready to serve.

" I remember the day Gabriella Versano and her husband Roberto moved onto our street in Overbrook. They were a young couple, looking to make a life in this new country just like the rest of us. They came with no family and so we quickly brought them into ours. We raised our children together and spent many holidays together. A family gathering would not be the same without her tiramisu. Gabriella has been by my side during the most challenging times in my life. I can call on her for anything, but in reality, I never have to, because she is always two steps ahead of me and knows when I need her to lift me up. During the last few years, she has given me her shoulder to cry on, but at the same time the strength to keep going. During the last few months of Francesco's life, she never left my side. And now, a day does not go by without a phone call, or a visit at work for a coffee and some chit chat. Whenever I want to give up, she pushes me forward. Words cannot describe the unconditional friendship, or better yet sisterhood, Gabriella and I share, and I am so grateful to have her in my life." – Elisa

TIRAMISU

MY RECIPE FOR MARRIAGE

Throughout this book I have shared stories about my life and the many inspirations that have influenced my style of preparing food—and, honestly, how I have lived my life. The village I came from, the family I grew up with, the journey to America, my life in this new world—I may not have realized the importance of these things at the time, but today, looking back, I would not trade any of it, the good nor the bad, for anything. I suppose a lot of people could say that about their lives.

Of all the things I have encountered in my life, there is one person whom I have not yet paid full tribute to. I was fortunate to be married to my best friend and soul mate, Francesco, for 55 years. We journeyed through so much together, and now I dedicate this book and everything in it to his memory.

As I have mentioned, Francesco and I met in Poggio Valle many, many years ago. When I first encountered Francesco, I had been seeing a young man for close to 4 years. I hesitate to call it dating, because we were so young and what did we know? This is the young man I met at the dance years before; the night I snuck away from my duties preparing meatballs for my family's Sunday dinner. This certain young man was kind and gentle, and I do not wish to be unkind, but he did not have many prospects when I knew him: no job and no interest in change. I will say that there were a number of men in our village and the surrounding area who were interested in befriending me, as they saw my American citizenship as a free ticket to the land of opportunity, which so many desperately wanted. I had to be careful with whom I associated, as there were, unfortunately, a few people with ulterior motives.

But this young man was nice enough. Truly, I never thought we would marry; I never got the feeling that this was the person with whom I should spend a lifetime. But we were happy enough to spend our free time together.

And then Francesco rode into town on his motorcycle looking for work. It seems almost a cliché from a Hollywood movie, but he was handsome and dashing, and he was a little rebellious and wild. He hailed from a village far away, a 2-hour ride each way on that little motorcycle. However, there was work to be had in Poggio Valle, and so he would dutifully ride all the way to our little town for work.

I was instantly taken by this handsome young man the first time I met him. He was a bricklayer, and at the time, the bricklayer trade was as respectable as that of a doctor because of the wage bricklayers earned. I have to say we became fast friends. We would have to sneak around to see each other, for my father certainly did not approve of this rebellious young soul, and the townspeople also did not trust him. We had a saying known to us: Donne e buoi, ai paesi suoi, which loosely translates as Women and cattle, from your own town. In other words, young men were supposed to find food and sustenance in their own hometown, and if they were smart, they would fall in love with and marry a young woman from their own village.

Francesco certainly knew this custom, but he was always a willful individual. He insisted and persisted in pursuing me. As I worked in the kitchen, he would sit outside a small window and we would talk, or he would visit the fountain for a drink of water just about the time of day I would be fetching water or washing clothes. We talked about a great many things, about dreams we both had for the future, about our childhoods, about our villages. This friendship soon grew into something much more. We fell in love and knew that we should spend our lives together.

At first, we were in no rush to marry. As I mentioned, my father never approved of Francesco, and he had been conducting his own search for a husband for me. At last through friends he learned of a young man in Rome from a family with means, who had a son, who by chance had eyes on America. My father figured, with my legal rights to American citizenship and his financial background, we could make a nice life together. So, with this being said, I tried to break the news to Francesco that my father had made arrangements for me to meet this man.

Sad and dejected, Francesco climbed aboard his motorcycle and rode all the way back to his hometown not knowing for sure what to make of all that had transpired. As I have mentioned, Francesco was willful, and perhaps a bit stubborn. After he rode all the way back home, he decided he was not satisfied with my attempt to end our relationship. And so, he climbed back aboard his motorcycle and rode another two hours back to Poggio Valle to speak to my father.

To hear my father tell this story, he was at our village church praying when Francesco burst in and asked him to come outside so they could talk. I honestly do not know the full substance of what they discussed, but eventually my father saw the persistence of this young man and came to appreciate his genuine feelings towards me, and so he relented. My mother and I were preparing dinner when my father entered the room with Francesco by his side.

This humble act was my father's way of permitting us to marry.

I will say that not everyone was pleased with my father's decision to consent. Some of the men in our town were furious and wanted to hurt (or kill) this young man who dared to take one of their women away. There was one day when Francesco found his motorcycle had been taken apart and the pieces left on a path leading out of town. I suspect I knew who was involved in this stunt, but really, so many years later, I am finally able to see the humor in this absurd childishness.

Our parents quickly met, and our wedding date was set. Our fathers decided a quick wedding would be best. Because of his age, by law, Francesco would be conscripted for a term of service in the army. Our fathers figured that because Francesco was an only son, which could pro-

tect him from service if he were married, that the army would not disturb a young family. We would have married eventually, but the thought of us being separated certainly spurred us to action.

After the marriage, we followed another Italian custom, and I went to live with my in-laws. Again, his whole family knew that Francesco should not bring a woman from another town to live with them, and his sisters were jealous of our relationship at first. But they put their concerns aside, stood up to the moans and groans of the town, and welcomed me with open arms. Francesco and I had a very intense fight soon after our wedding; I am sure we disagreed many times over the years about particular things, but the details have slipped away as inconsequential. But I will never forget when I bellowed at him that we should never have married. Ah, but we were young, and so given to our passions that even this memory does not cloud the many good ones we shared over the years.

At the time, however, to say that life was not easy is an understatement. Yet, I did my duty as a housewife and daughter-in-law and prepared all the meals and did the cleaning as I was expected to do. I was not always happy, but I was ultimately together with Francesco, and so it was bearable.

Despite our plan, the army called Francesco to serve his term and off he went to Northern Italy for eighteen months. I was expected to live in this foreign village, pregnant with my first child, with a village who barely tolerated me, and who expected me to be the dutiful daughter-in-law. These were perhaps the hardest times of our lives. I have many difficult memories from this period, but, again, these years were formative in my life, and so I am able to look past the slights and insults to see that his village was simply trying to protect Francesco.

I think, by this point, you will know of our journey in the new world together, of raising a family, of struggling together, and of enduring hardships and heartbreak, but in the end, always winding up exactly where we wanted to be, Francesco and I always together until the very end.

Francesco grew very ill very suddenly at the end of his life, but we got to spend every day of it together. This is when Francesco joined me in the kitchen, and we shared the last months of his life cooking and preparing food together. It felt like old times again; here I was toiling away in the kitchen, and Francesco, instead of being outside a small window, sat a few feet away from me so that we could talk and share.

We talked about a great many things in those moments. But this time, we did not talk about the future, but about the past. We did not dream of all the things we wanted to do; instead, we recalled all that we had lived through together. We laughed as we shared stories, and we cried as we thought about friends and family no longer with us.

Just like those innocent conversations so many years before in Poggio Valle, these times together grew into something so much more. I was able to fall in love all over again, and, of all the memories I have in my lifetime, the one I hold most dear are the times I got to share with the love of my life sharing my passion of cooking.

To Francesco. We are together always in spirit …

TRADITIONAL MENUS

Christmas Eve Dinner
Chickpea Soup
Clams Casino Fried Smelts
Spaghetti Cioppino
Sautéed Baccalà
Broiled Baccalà

Christmas Day
Antipasti
Italian Wedding Soup
or Scrippelle Mbusse
Spaghetti
Timballo
Chicken Cutlets
Meatballs and Sausage
Roast Lamb
Assortment of Side Dishes
Italian Rum Cake
and Homemade Cookies

Easter Day
Antipasti
Escarole Soup
Ravioli
Timballo
Lamb Cutlets
Lamb Stew
Roasted Lamb
Assortment of Side Dishes
Easter Bread and Chocolate Eggs

New Year's Eve Dinner
Antipasti
Lentil Soup
Timballo
Roast Pork
Assortment of Side Dishes
Italian Rum Cake

New Year's Day
Antipasti
Escarole Soup
Ravioli
Timballo
Lamb Cutlets
Lamb Stew
Roasted Lamb
Assortment of Side Dishes
Ricotta Cheesecake and Impossible Pie

Thanksgiving Day
Antipasti
Escarole Soup
Spaghetti
Timballo
Meatballs and Sausage
Roasted Turkey
Roasted Lamb
Assortment of Side Dishes
Ricotta Cheesecake and Impossible Pie

Carnevale

BREAKFAST

Fresh eggs, sausage, and bacon with bread

MID-MORNING

Fried Dough

LUNCH

Ravioli with Sugar – Ravioli Dolce

MID AFTERNOON

Fresh sliced cheese and sausage
spread over fresh bread

SUNDOWN

Scrippelle Mbusse

DINNER

Roasted Lamb or Filet

LATE SNACK

Pappardelle with cheese and butter

DESSERTS

Cicerchiata and Frappe

Traditional Italian Wedding Celebration

Antipasti

Italian Wedding Soup

Spaghetti alla Chitarra

Timballo

Beef Genovese

Roasted Chicken

Veal Cutlets

Roasted Lamb

Assortment of Side Dishes

Italian Rum Cake

"Celebrated on the eve of Ash Wednesday, this tradition dates back to the 1400's when Italian people would feast on many meals throughout the day in order to prepare for the fasting required by the Catholic Church during the Lenten season. This is what I remember my mother preparing for our family." - Elisa

INDEX

Liquid Measures

1 gal = 4 qt = 8 pt = 16 cups = 128 fl oz
½ gal = 2 qt = 4 pt = 8 cups = 64 fl oz
¼ gal = 1 qt = 2 pt = 4 cups = 32 fl oz
½ qt = 1 pt = 2 cups = 16 fl oz
¼ qt = ½ pt = 1 cup = 8 fl oz

Dry Measures

1 cup = 16 Tbsp = 48 tsp = 250ml
¾ cup = 12 Tbsp = 36 tsp = 175ml
⅔ cup = 10 ⅔ Tbsp = 32 tsp = 150ml
½ cup = 8 Tbsp = 24 tsp = 125ml
⅓ cup = 5 ⅓ Tbsp = 16 tsp = 75ml
¼ cup = 4 Tbsp = 12 tsp = 50ml
⅛ cup = 2 Tbsp = 6 tsp = 30ml
1 Tbsp = 3 tsp = 15ml

Dash or Pinch or Speck = less than ⅛ tsp

Quickies

1 fl oz = 30 ml
1 oz = 28.35 g
1 lb = 16 oz (454 g)
1 kg = 2.2 lb
1 quart = 2 pints

U.S.	Metric
¼ tsp	1.25 mL
½ tsp	2.5 mL
1 tsp	5 mL
1 Tbl	15 mL
¼ cup	50 mL
⅓ cup	75 mL
½ cup	125 mL
⅔ cup	150 mL
¾ cup	175 mL
1 cup	250 mL
1 quart	1 liter

Recipe Abbreviations

Cup = c or C
Fluid = fl
Gallon = gal
Ounce = oz
Package = pkg
Pint = pt
Pound = lb or #
Quart = qt
Square = sq
Tablespoon = T or Tbl
          or TBSP or TBS
Teaspoon = t or tsp

Fahrenheit (°F) to Celcius (°C)
°C = (°F - 32) x 5/9

32°F	0°C
40°F	4°C
140°F	60°C
150°F	65°C
160°F	70°C
225°F	107°C
250°F	121°C
275°F	135°C
300°F	150°C
325°F	165°C
350°F	177°C
375°F	190°C
400°F	205°C
425°F	220°C
450°F	230°C
475°F	245°C
500°F	260°C

OVEN TEMPERATURES

WARMING: 200°F
VERY SLOW: 250°F - 275°F
SLOW: 300°F - 325°F
MODERATE: 350°F - 375°F
HOT: 400°F - 425°F
VERY HOT: 450°F - 475°F

*Some measurements were rounded

IN THE END

I have no regrets. God has decided my immediate family should go from five to three and so I go on living, sometimes questioning, but enjoying the time I have left with my family and friends. My husband has left our surviving children the memories of his art by constructing them two of the most beautiful kitchens I have ever seen. And now I have given them a collection of my art that they, their children and their grandchildren will share in those kitchens. So, in essence, when it is my time to be reunited with Francesco and my daughter Agnes, we will all continue to be together in a special way, gathered around the table surrounded by both our legacies and the most important gift of all, Love.